THE WORLD BANK

Kohn Pedersen Fox
and the Architecture of a Landmark Building

By John Morris Dixon, FAIA

THE WORLD BANK

Headquarters Building
Washington, DC

By Kohn Pedersen Fox Associates PC,
Architects and Planning Consultants

First published in Australia in 2002 by
The Images Publishing Group Pty Ltd
ACN 059 734 431
6 Bastow Place, Mulgrave, Victoria 3170, Australia
Telephone (+61 3) 9561 5544 Facsimile (+61 3) 9561 4860
email: books@images.com.au
www.imagespublishinggroup.com

Copyright © The Images Publishing Group Pty Ltd, 2002
The Images Publishing Group Reference Number: 256

All rights reserved. Apart from any fair dealing for the purposes of private study, research, criticism or review as permitted under the Copyright Act, no part of this publication may be reproduced, stored in a retrieval system or transmitted in any form by any means, electronic, mechanical, photocopying, recording or otherwise, without the written permission of the publisher.

National Library of Australia Cataloguing-in-Publication Data

The World Bank.
Dixon, John Morris.

ISBN 1 875498 90 7

1. World Bank. 2. Bank buildings – Washington (D.C.). 3. Architecture, Modern – 20th century – Washington (D.C.).

725.2409753

Graphic Co-ordinator: Ilona Rider assisted by Puja Kutwal

Designed by The Graphic Image Studio Pty Ltd
Mulgrave, Australia

Film by Pageset Pty Ltd, Australia
Printed in China by Everbest Printing

IMAGES has included on its website a page for special notices in relation to this and our other publications. It includes updates to the information printed in our books.
Please visit this site: www.imagespublishinggroup.com

Members of the World Bank design team gather with bank president
after William Pedersen's presentation of the winning design.
Around model of proposed building are (left to right):
Jerrily R. Kress, of KressCox Associates, Associate Architects;
William Pedersen and A. Eugene Kohn of Kohn Pedersen Fox Associates, Architects;
Barber B. Conable, president of the World Bank;
Sheldon Fox, principal of Kohn Pedersen Fox Associates.

CONTENTS

Preface   9

Introduction   10

Design   20
    Need for a New Headquarters   20
    Architect Selection by Competition   23
    KPF Shapes the World Bank   26
        First Competition Design
        Final Competition Design

Structural/Mechanical Systems   50

Construction Process   54

Building Envelope   64
    Evolution of KPF Curtain Walls   64
    Design of World Bank Curtain Walls   66

Specific Spaces   74
    Entrance and Lobby   74
    Atrium   78
    Typical Offices   98
    Special Spaces   104
        Auditorium
        Executive Directors' Board Room
        Executive Directors' Conference Room
    Cafeteria   116
    Other Below-Grade Spaces   122

Finishes/Furnishings   124

Art Program   128

Final Evaluation   134

Credits   142

Acknowledgments   144

PREFACE

It is often said that architecture is a mirror of society. This implies that the role of the architect is to deal with "what is" rather than "what can be." In the design of the World Bank we rejected this traditional view in favor of an approach that brought about a physical transformation of the institution. The building became a new and unforeseen embodiment of its collective community.

It gives me tremendous satisfaction to walk into the courtyard here and watch the vibrancy of human interaction taking place. It has truly become the "town square" we had envisioned, enabling activities of many kinds to take place, often simultaneously.

The great American architect Louis Kahn said that the first duty of the architect is "to change the program." This always seemed a bit presumptuous to my ears, but the motivation was sound. What we have done here, perhaps, is to augment the program, rather than to change it. Regardless of how we define our role, the employees of the bank seem to enjoy the way this building has transformed their daily lives.

William Pedersen, FAIA

INTRODUCTION

Rarely does an organization of worldwide importance acquire a home that matches its aspirations. The odds are against it. The higher the organization's profile, the greater the pressure to please everyone. Fear of displaying too much independence often leads to a predictable monumentality that, ironically, pleases hardly anybody.

The Washington, DC, headquarters of the World Bank, an international agency for the support of economic growth in developing countries, unequivocally beats those odds. Designed by Kohn Pedersen Fox Associates with a slate of distinguished collaborators, it is a building that meets its owners' aspirations in several vital ways: it accommodates a vast and varied program of high-quality working spaces within a restricted volume; it presents to the world an image that is distinguished, yet blessedly free of monumentality or material excess; it fits into the built pattern of Washington without surrendering to design conformity. In a city where too many recent buildings abjectly concede to convention, its creative, internationally oriented design is inspiring.

Several factors favored a better-than-routine architectural design for the World Bank. The bank already controlled an entire city block in a prime location fronting on Pennsylvania Avenue, which could accommodate a far greater volume of offices than the motley group of

1 North side of final competition model, seen from Pennsylvania Avenue.
2 Rendering of building seen from Pennsylvania Avenue, final competition design.
Following pages:
Completed building, seen from Pennsylvania Avenue.

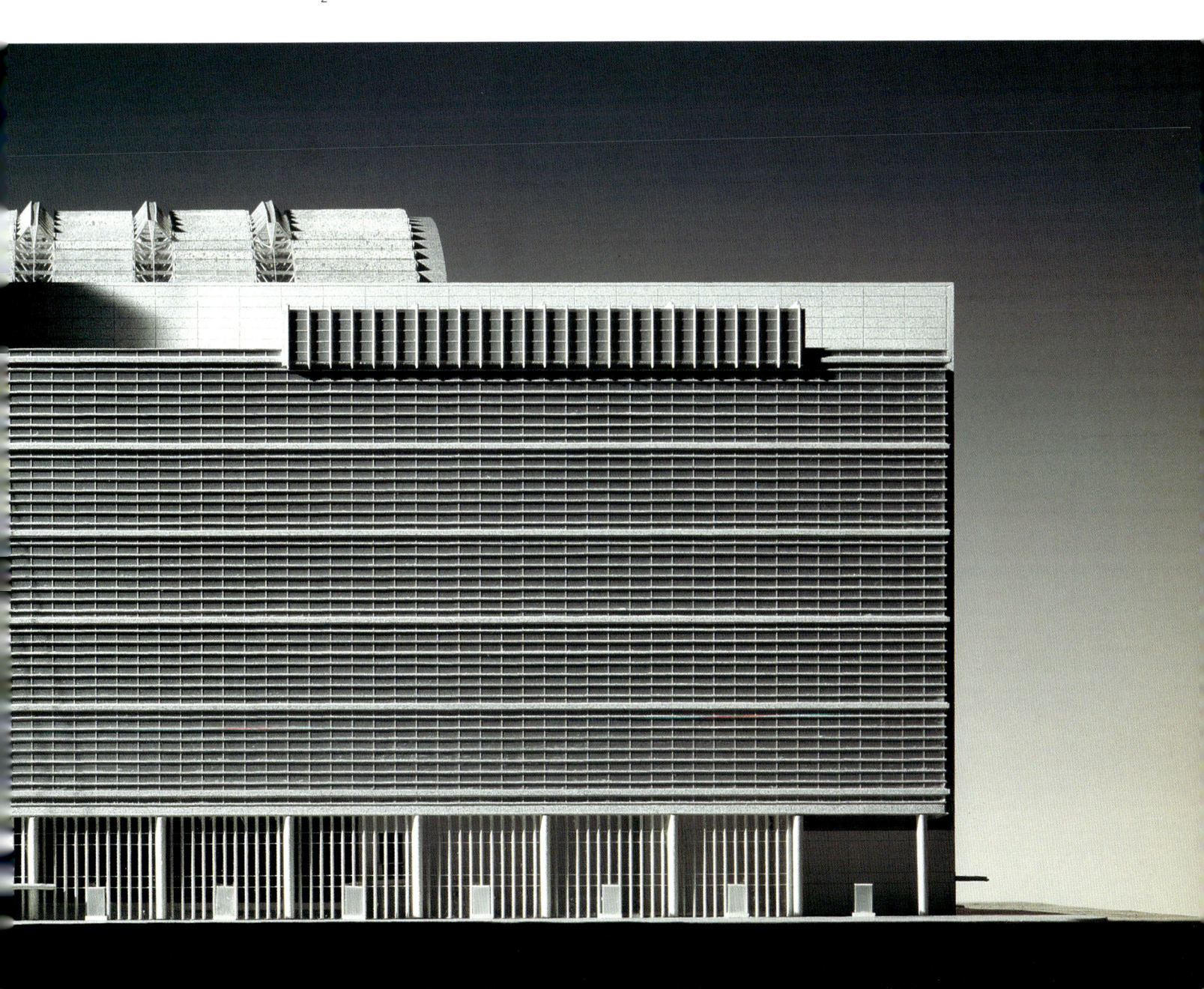

2

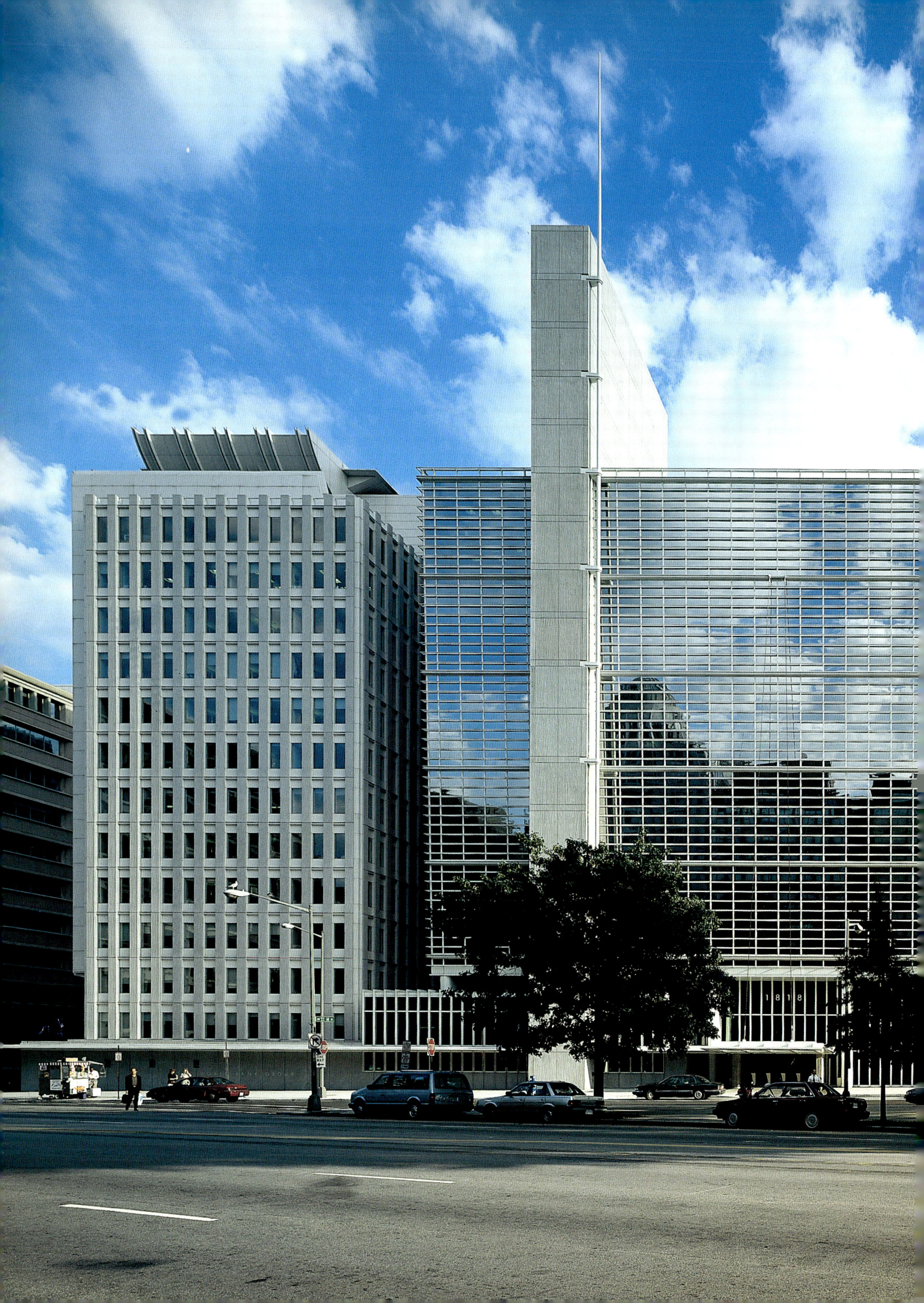
1818

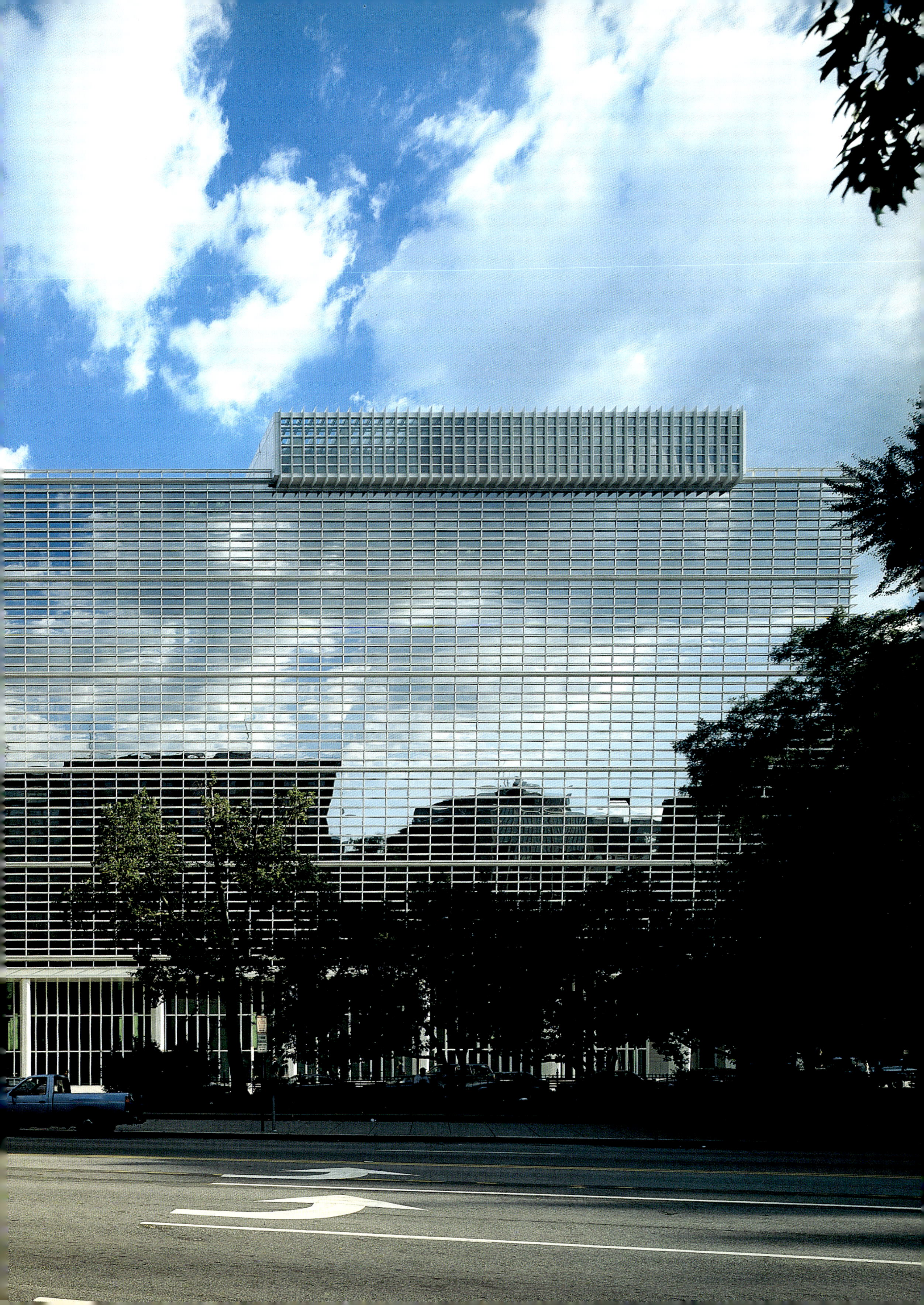

4 Completed building from northwest corner, showing existing E Building, at right, incorporated into complex.

5 Completed building from northeast corner, showing existing D Building, at left, incorporated into complex.

structures the bank then occupied. Its international nature virtually necessitated a rational, international search for an architect. An architect selection process was developed by which some 76 participants from 26 countries submitted their qualifications, then eight were chosen to submit competitive designs.

While seven of these proposals envisioned replacing every structure on the block, in a phased sequence, only the team headed by Kohn Pedersen Fox Associates proposed permanently retaining the two most modern buildings and integrating them into a full-block development.

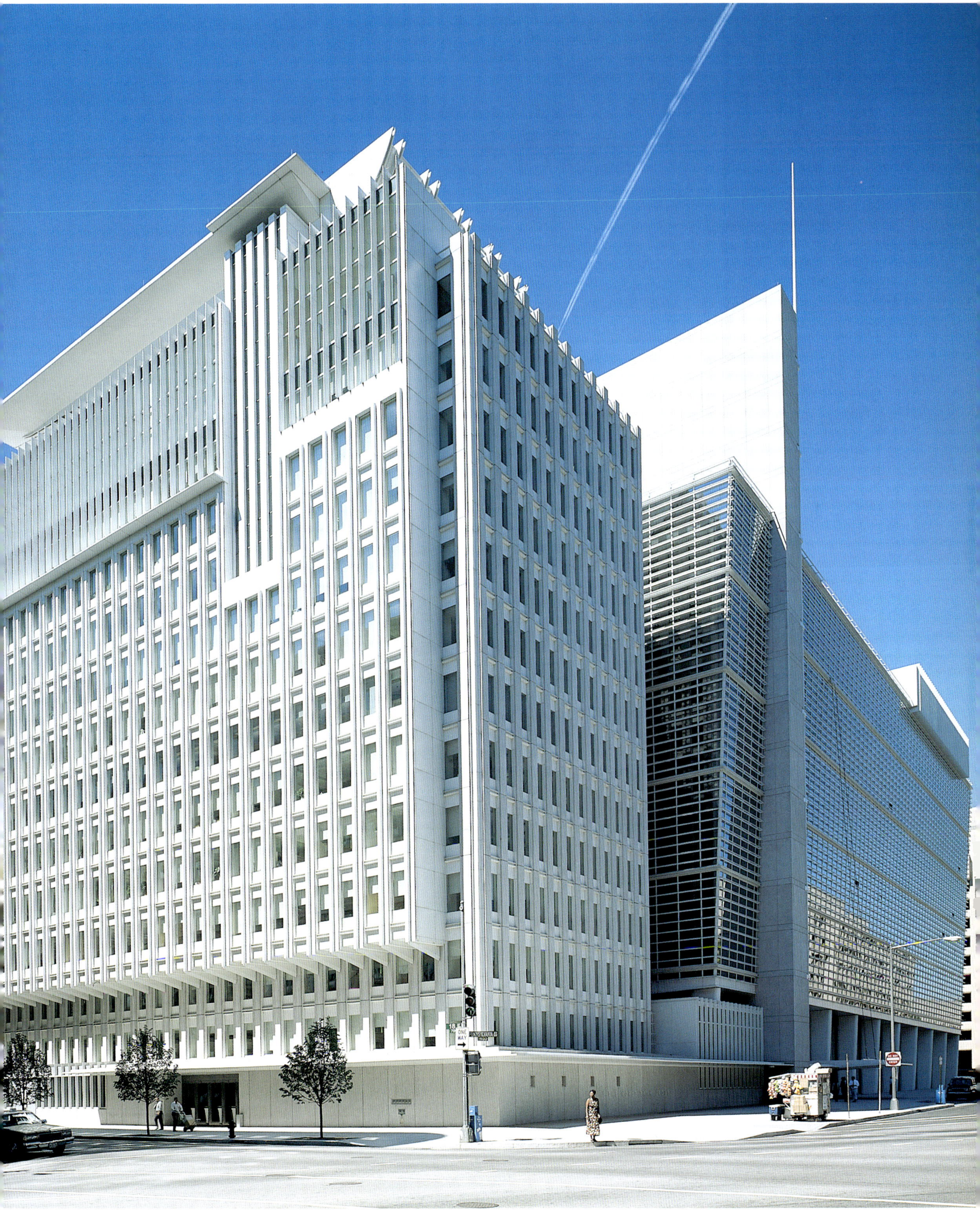

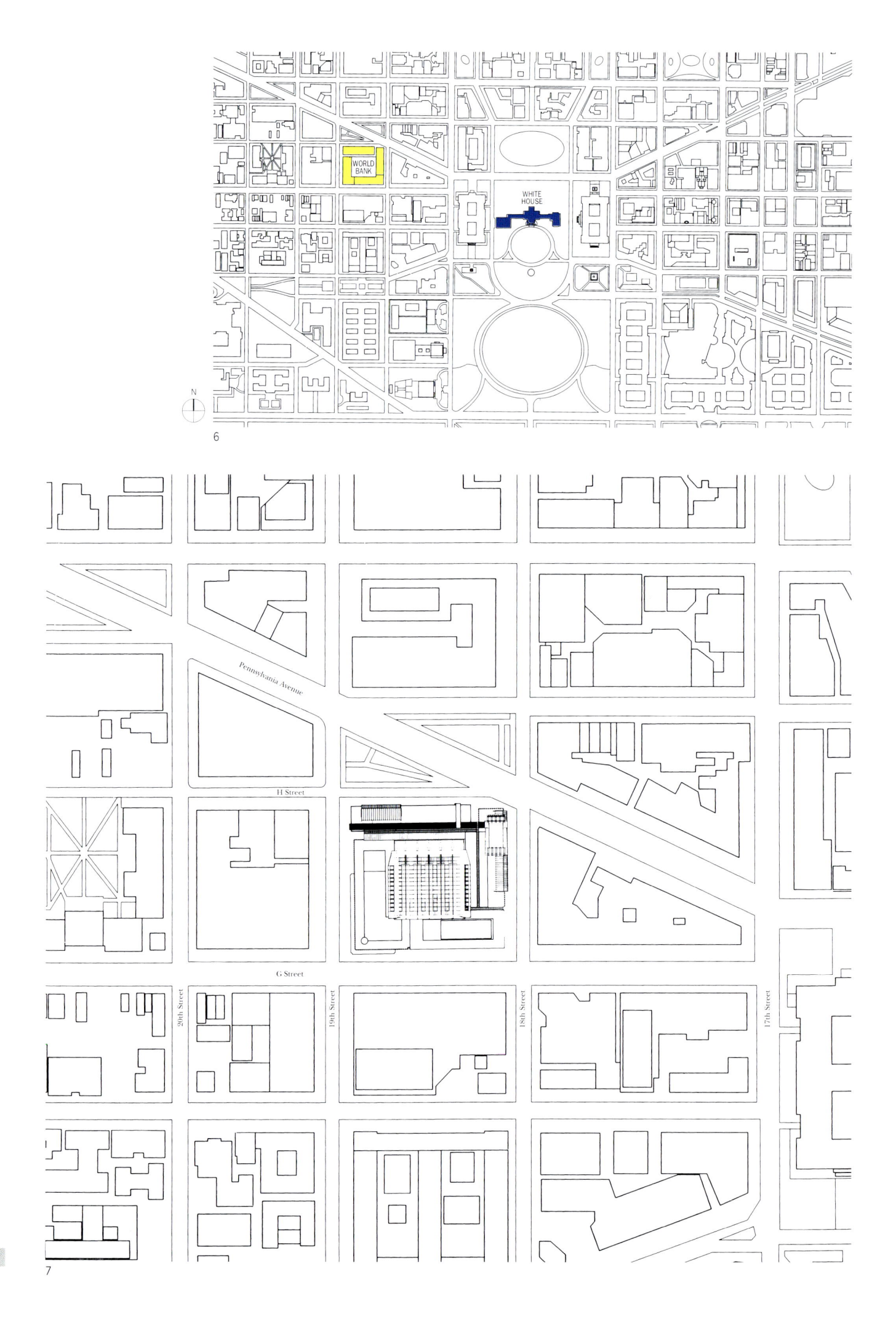

6

7

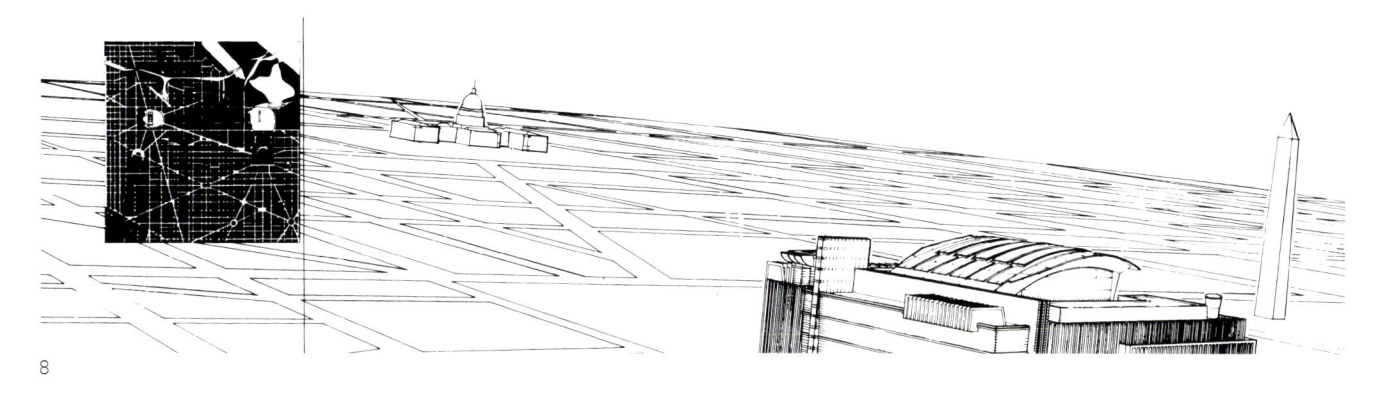

The advantages of this scheme were apparent in terms of shortening construction time, by years, and reduced disruption of operations. But these procedural advantages were hardly the only virtues of the design. It also offered a mid-block enclosed atrium, which would provide an attractive resting/gathering place but also a view from surrounding offices that is equal to—in some respects better than—those enjoyed from offices facing the surrounding streets. What's more, the design was distinguished by innumerable sensitive decisions in the shaping of its volumes, the sequence of its interior spaces, the treatment of its surfaces, the refinement of its work spaces, and many other aspects that make the resulting building an example to be studied.

The $314-million complex contains 2.1 million square feet, about 900,000 in the existing buildings and 1.2 million in new construction. It accommodates 4,300 employees, a 35 percent increase over the number previously housed on the site. Of the total square-footage, 30 percent is below street level, responding to Washington's 130-foot height limit. The structure does not appear monolithic or daunting, because the very concept of KPF's design is to break up the overall volume visually into an ensemble of buildings, at the scale of the two buildings the architects retained on the site.

6   Location map, portion of Washington, with White House at center, World Bank to northwest, highlighted.
7   Roof plan of World Bank, with surrounding streets.
8   Diagrammatic perspective of Washington, showing World Bank in foreground, Capitol at left, and Washington Monument at right.
9   Rooftop-level view, showing World Bank in setting, looking east.
10 Aerial view of city, with top of World Bank highlighted.
11 Rooftop-level view looking southwest.
12 Rooftop-level view looking south.

17

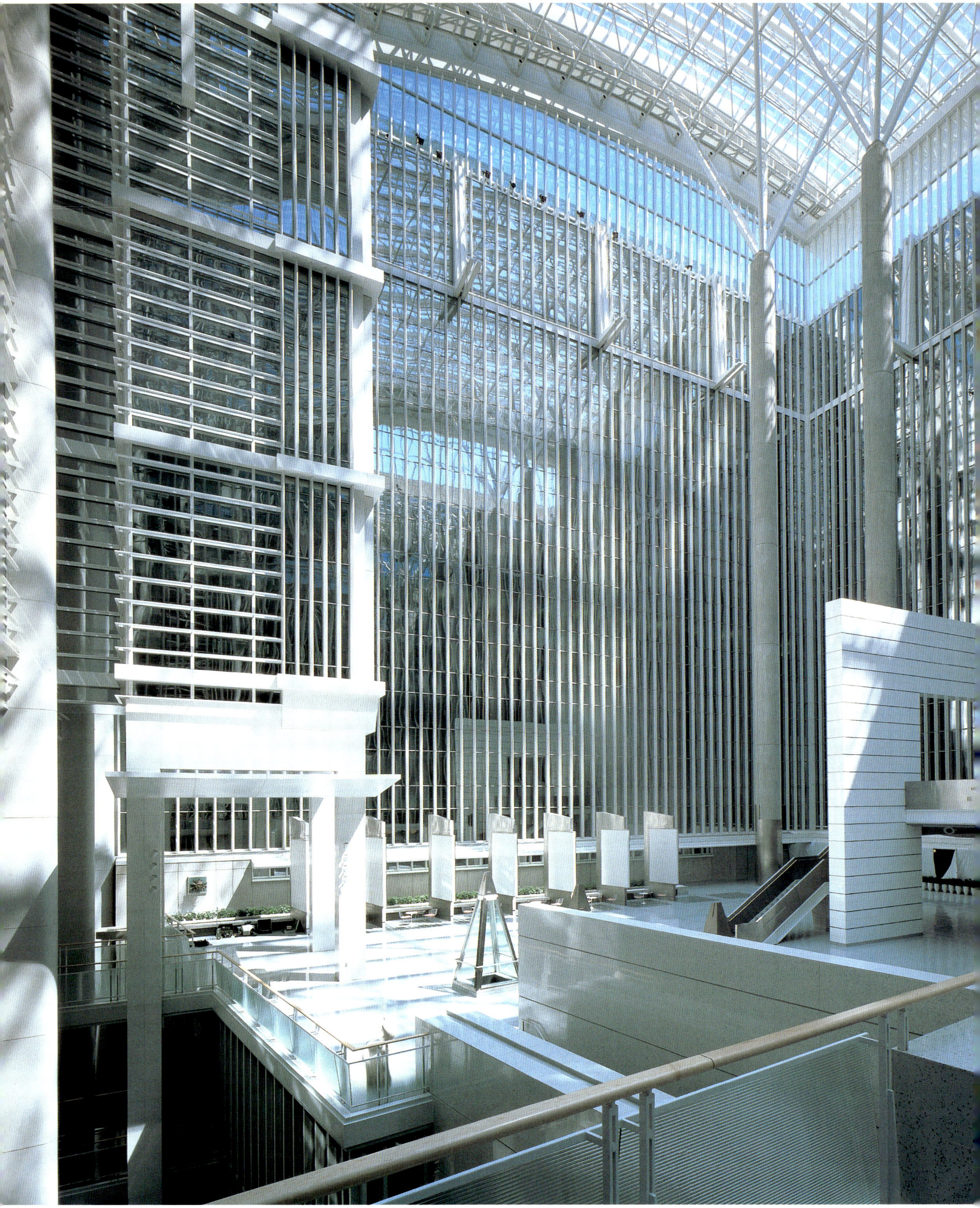

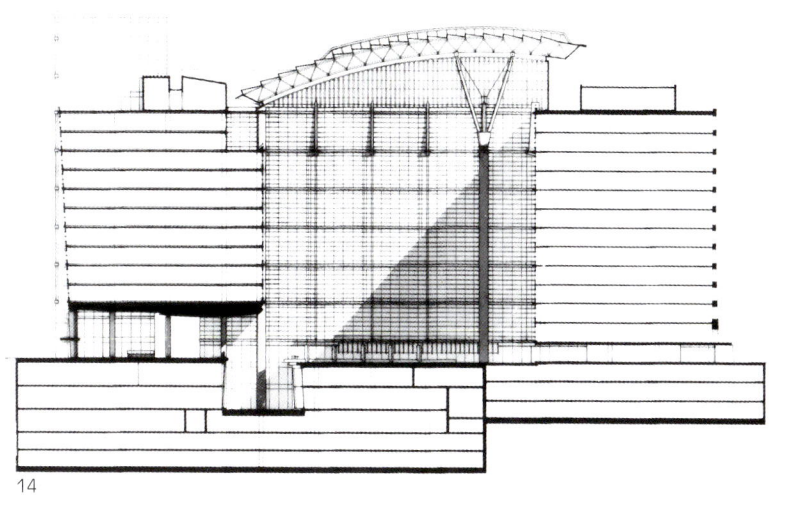

In the design stage, KPF's scheme was widely praised and won a coveted P/A Awards Citation. Completed, with hardly any alterations of the competition design, the building won New York City, New York State, and national Honor Awards from the American Institute of Architects. Few buildings have so impressed fellow architects as to win all of these honors.

This book is an exploration of the design and engineering ideas, large and small, that make this building outstanding. For all those who aspire to design excellence, it should be an exploration worth making.

13 Central atrium from raised terrace.
14 Section through building looking east, showing central atrium.

DESIGN

Need for a New Headquarters

Phase 1 | Phase 2

1

The World Bank's first office was opened in 1946 in a building dating from 1941 at 1818 H Street, two blocks from the White House. In stages, the bank had expanded to fill five other buildings on the same city block. The oldest was built in 1921. The most recent ones were the E Building, completed in 1967 and acquired by the bank in 1973, and the D Building, completed to the bank's specifications in 1969. In 1984, the bank acquired the last narrow parcel between two of its buildings to complete ownership of the entire block.

The existing buildings were inherently inefficient. Since some were considerably smaller than would be permitted under zoning, the bank's total floor area was only about 85 percent of the allowable on the site. The division between buildings made many of the floors too small for effective layout of departments. At several points, floor levels between buildings did not align, so that connections between departments could be tortuous, in some cases achieved only through mazelike corridors that had evolved. Lighting and mechanical systems were largely obsolescent. The older buildings were hard to adapt to modern communications technology. Building security was difficult to maintain in the disjointed complex with numerous entrances. Fire safety did not meet current standards: the structures lacked sprinklers, and their mechanical systems could promote the spread of smoke and fumes.

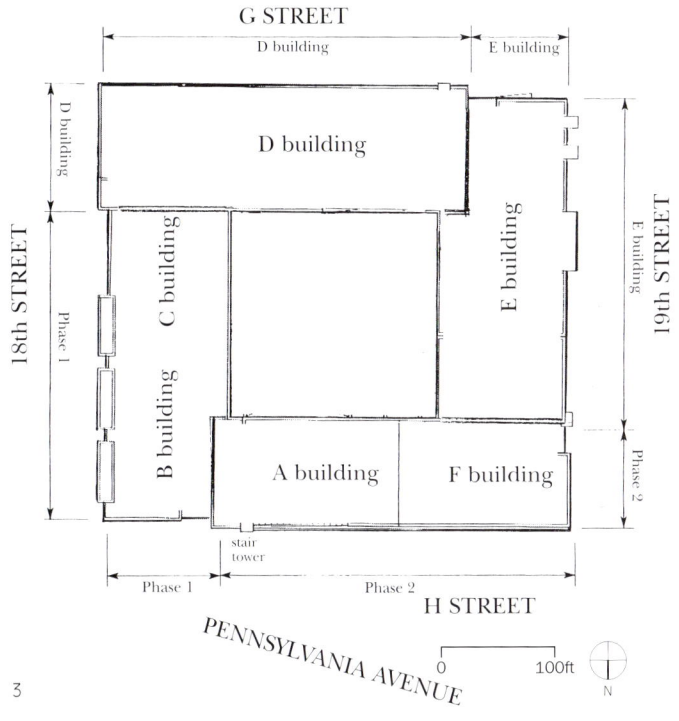

Retrofit of existing buildings, alone, could have corrected the most basic problems of fire safety, air quality, power supply, and communications capability, but could not make the floor areas efficient or the layout of departments convenient. Nor would that allow the bank to maximize building area on its land, thus decreasing dependence on leased space.

Studies of various options for improving and/or replacing the bank's offices date back to the early 1980s. Total or partial moves to the suburbs were among the many options considered, but more intense development on the same site was never ruled out, because larger floor areas and more efficient layouts could substantially increase the workforce accommodated there. New buildings, moreover, could provide several more floors of below-ground space, to accommodate parking and such centralized facilities as the print shop, the medical facilities, library, and the staff cafeteria. Altogether a new headquarters on the site was projected to house over 4,300 staff members (450 of them in below-grade departments), compared to about 3,200 in the existing buildings.

1 Front of previous World Bank buildings on H Street, facing north toward Pennsylvania Avenue.
2 Open court at center of previous World Bank complex.
3 Diagrammatic plan of previous World Bank buildings, showing locations of Buildings A through F and Phases 1 and 2 of new construction.

In 1989 it was decided that a new complex should be developed on the full-block site. Among the bank's objectives cited then, in addition to relieving functional deficiencies and expanding usable square footage, was to "act as a responsible member of the local community."

As for the architecture of its new headquarters, the World Bank's status as an international organization argued for holding an international design competition. The primary goal of any design competition is the identification of the best professional team to design the project. But there is almost always the equally important goal of assigning the selection of the architects to a panel of experts whose judgment is unlikely to be questioned. Such a fair and informed selection process was especially apt for an organization led by people from various countries, in many of which design competitions are customary for choosing architects even for modest buildings.

The bank's in-house facilities team, including some architects, worked with outside consultants to draw up procedures for a design competition and a program to guide competitors. It was a three-stage procedure involving three different expert panels: a screening committee to select teams to participate in the competition, a technical review committee to study and report on the entries, and an evaluation panel to consider the technical review report along with the design presentation by the competing teams, then recommend a final selection to bank management. Instead of carrying out the competition under the long-established rules of the UIA (International Union of Architects), in which entries remain anonymous throughout the process, the bank elected to follow the more recently accepted practice—more common in the United States than elsewhere—of having competing teams make in-person presentations of their work to the final evaluation panel.

The competition program called for a new building to be completed in three phases in somewhat more than six years:

Phase 1: New construction to replace the B and C Buildings with a structure of about 450,000 square feet.

Phase 2: New construction to replace the A and F Buildings and the basements below the block's central courtyard with a structure of about 750,000 square feet.

Phase 3: Retrofit of the bank's two 1960's buildings (D and E Buildings).

Though the competition program included modernization of the D and E Buildings, least obsolescent of the six, competitors were asked to draw up a master plan for their eventual replacement, in a fourth phase not yet scheduled.

Phasing of construction was necessary, in order to limit the displacement of bank staff at any one time—and to recognize the limited amount of "swing space" the bank could lease nearby during the construction process. Another key consideration was that a new central mechanical plant would have to be completed and working in Phase 1 before the existing mechanical facilities were demolished to make room for Phase 2.

In the competition program, the bank stressed its need for a design that would "facilitate flexible and systematic office rearrangement to accommodate frequent staff moves and organizational changes, while maximizing the space use efficiency." Capacity to incorporate the latest information technology was also stressed. "Improved access to natural light" for offices was essential, particularly since a high percentage of the bank's staff come from nations where natural light in the workplace was considered essential, as compared to the acceptance of deep, artificially lighted workplaces in the United States. In order to maximize exposure to daylight, it was suggested that the completed complex incorporate three glass-enclosed atriums, although competitors were encouraged to "improve on these ideas."

Architect Selection by Competition

Initially, notice of the competition was distributed worldwide through architectural organizations, advertisements in journals, and offices of the bank's executive directors. As a result, more than 300 firms requested the competition prospectus and information on submitting qualifications. Actually submitting qualifications information to the screening committee were 76 teams from 26 countries, many of them consortiums of more than one firm.

The screening committee considering these qualifications comprised three members from the bank staff, including staff architects, and three independent experts. They ranked all competitors according to consistent criteria, and recommended eight teams to bank management.

The selected teams were:
Arthur Erickson Architects, a Canadian firm that had recently completed the Canadian Embassy in Washington, and HTB/DMJM, a United States joint venture, which had recently completed the National Press Club building in Washington.

Cannon Corporation, a United States firm with broad international experience, with Moriyama & Teshima Architects, of Canada, and Dissing and Weitling, a Danish firm founded by Arne Jacobsen, pioneer Danish designer.

Edward Larrabee Barnes/John M.Y. Lee & Partners, a New York firm that had recently won the design competition for the Judiciary Office Building in Washington.

Hellmuth, Obata & Kassabaum (HOK), a United States firm, architects of the Air and Space Museum in Washington, and Kajima Corporation, a Japanese architecture/engineering firm with worldwide experience.

John Andrews International, the Australian firm that designed the Intelsat headquarters in Washington.

Kohn Pedersen Fox Associates, a New York firm with international experience, and KressCox Associates, a Washington firm, with Naegele, Hofmann, Tiedemann, a West German design firm.

Norconsult International, a Norwegian consulting firm with wide international experience, with Platou Architects, a distinguished Norwegian design firm, and Lund & Slaatto Architects, a Norwegian firm with extensive experience with the Bank of Norway.

Skidmore, Owings & Merrill (SOM), the United States firm that designed the D Building, and Nihon Sekkei, one of Japan's leading architectural firms, with Charles Correa, renowned Indian architect, serving as design consultant.

The eight finalists were noticeably weighted toward North American firms, with five teams led by United States firms, one by a Canadian architect—all of them noted for the design of large office buildings as part of a wide-ranging practice. Participation by firms from some countries may have been influenced by the fact that the competition did not follow the procedure recommended by the International Union of Architects (UIA) and therefore did not have its endorsement. The screening committee's choices were undoubtedly influenced by the stated criteria they were to apply, which included, among other qualifications: experience relevant to this commission (in type, size, complexity of projects), international experience, and the ability to provide professional services in Washington. Recognizing the bank's interest in

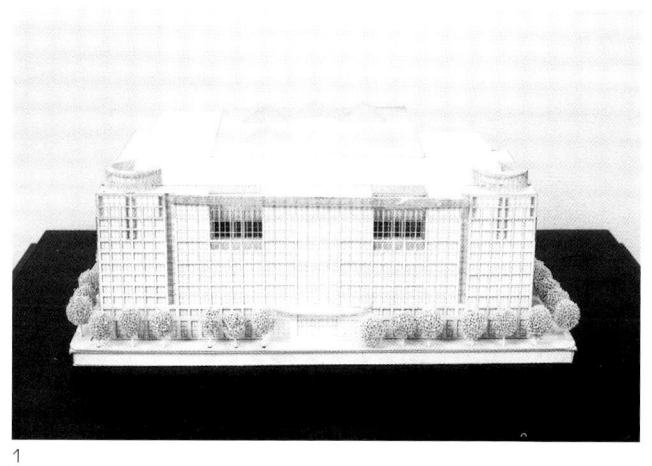

1. Skidmore, Owings & Merrill competition model.
2. Norconsult International competition model.
3. Edward Larrabee Barnes/John M. Y. Lee competition model.
4. Hellmuth, Obata & Kassabaum competition model.

international participation, many of the teams submitting included architects from more than one country, so that in all 10 countries were represented among the eight finalist teams.

After they had received design program material, all eight teams participated in a week-long site orientation at the World Bank in July 1989. Teams had to submit entries in a prescribed format on October 20. These were examined by the technical review committee, which included a representative of the construction management firm the bank had already commissioned (Sverdrup/Gilbane/Hanscomb). Criteria included adherence to the bank's program, cost, constructability, and design of mechanical systems.

During a two-week period in October and November, the teams were each given half a day to present their proposals in person before the evaluation panel. This group was structured to include five architects (one academician, one Washington-based, three "internationally based"), one expert on interior design and human factors, and three representatives of the bank (one executive director, one at vice president level, and one from the advisory committee for the project.)

This panel submitted a report, with recommendations, to the bank management, which made the final choice. Each team of designers received a $60,000 fee for their participation.

5

6

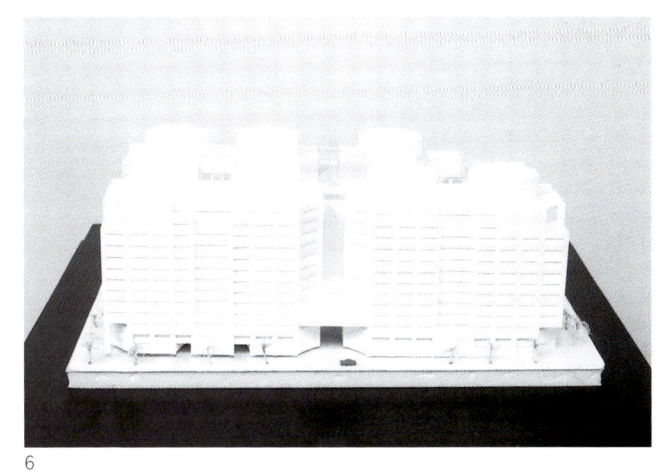

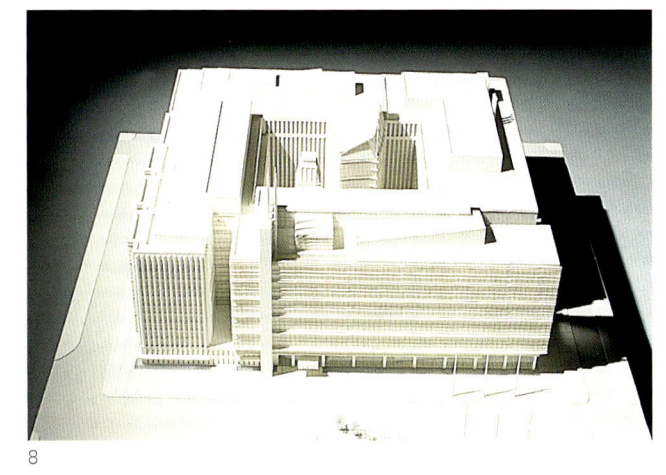

7

8

Members of the bank's evaluation panel were:

Yoshinobu Ashihara, an architect and professor of architecture, Japan

John de Monchaux, an Australian national and Dean of the School of Architecture and Planning at M.I.T.

Jean Nouvel, a noted French architect

Ranjit Sabikhi, an architect from India

George White, the Architect of the Capitol, Washington

John Zeisel, a United States human factors specialist

S. Shahid Husain, the bank's Vice President for the Latin American and Caribbean Region, chair of the panel

Everardo Wessels, Director, Technical Department, Latin American and Caribbean Region, and the chair of the bank's advisory committee for the project

Jacques de Groote, an executive director of the bank

In February 1990, this panel recommended the team led by Kohn Pedersen Fox Associates, and bank management awarded them the commission.

5   Arthur Erickson competition model.
6   John Andrews competition model.
7   Cannon Design, with Moriyama & Teshima, competition model.
8   Kohn Pedersen Fox competition model.

KPF Shapes the World Bank

1 Early sketch of final competition design.

Among the competing designs for the World Bank designs, the Kohn Pedersen Fox (KPF) team's stood out for several reasons. It was the only one that proposed permanently retaining the two most up-to-date buildings on the headquarters block: the D Building, designed by Skidmore, Owings & Merrill, and the E Building by Vincent Kling, both dating from the 1960s. The competition program had prescribed three scheduled phases of construction and renovation, to be followed at some undetermined future date by the replacement of these remaining buildings as part of an overall master plan. Only the KPF team proposed reusing these existing buildings and thoroughly integrating them, with alterations that went beyond mere stop-gap renovation, into the total development.

Preserving the two existing buildings not only cut several years off the original completion schedule, but it greatly reduced the disruption of staff activities and saved the cost and inconvenience of renting additional space off site. Moreover, due to KPF's inspired design efforts, the completed complex suffered not at all from incorporating the older buildings. In fact, KPF used the dimensions, surface characteristics, and placement of these existing structures—respectable works of their time, though not of landmark caliber—as starting points for a scheme that incorporates a series of harmonious building volumes ranged around the block in a pinwheel composition, enclosing a dramatic square atrium. Instead of an "object" building occupying the entire block, which would have been too monumental for this purpose, the bank has been shaped into a very effective series of architectural elements in the Washington cityscape. The image of an assemblage of parts making up a varied but coherent whole is seen as emblematic of the bank's multinational composition and mission.

Another feature unique to the KPF design is the way it maximized the amount of space the bank could occupy within Washington's 130-foot height limitation. Through close coordination with their structural and mechanical consultants, the architects were able to fit 13 floors, instead of the usual 12, within the 130-foot limit. This was accomplished by using post-tensioned concrete floor slabs and devising a vertical distribution of mechanical services, with only short horizontal runs, so that 8-foot 1-inch ceiling heights could be achieved within a 10-foot 1¼-inch floor-to-floor height. Altogether, the KPF design provides 1.2 million square feet of floor area in the completed complex.

Beneath street level, creative engineering allowed for five levels of below-grade facilities rather than the three usually considered the maximum because of Washington's high water table. Programmed spaces on these lower levels include libraries, archives, a credit union, employee health services, a mail room, and other common facilities, as well as staff dining spaces seating 1,500. Below the three levels of occupied facilities are parking spaces for 500 cars. To maximize usable area, some of the bank's underground spaces extend out to the curb, precluding in-the-ground planting for much of the surrounding sidewalks. The aluminum panels on the street level frontage of the complex are actually emergency egress and access points required for the substantial below-grade occupancy.

KPF's initial competition design, while similar to the executed scheme, had an open central court, rather than a covered atrium, which was introduced when the bank's evaluation panel asked KPF to return with a revised design for their consideration. Rather than choosing a

2&3 Early sketches for first and final competition designs, showing possible configurations considered by design team.

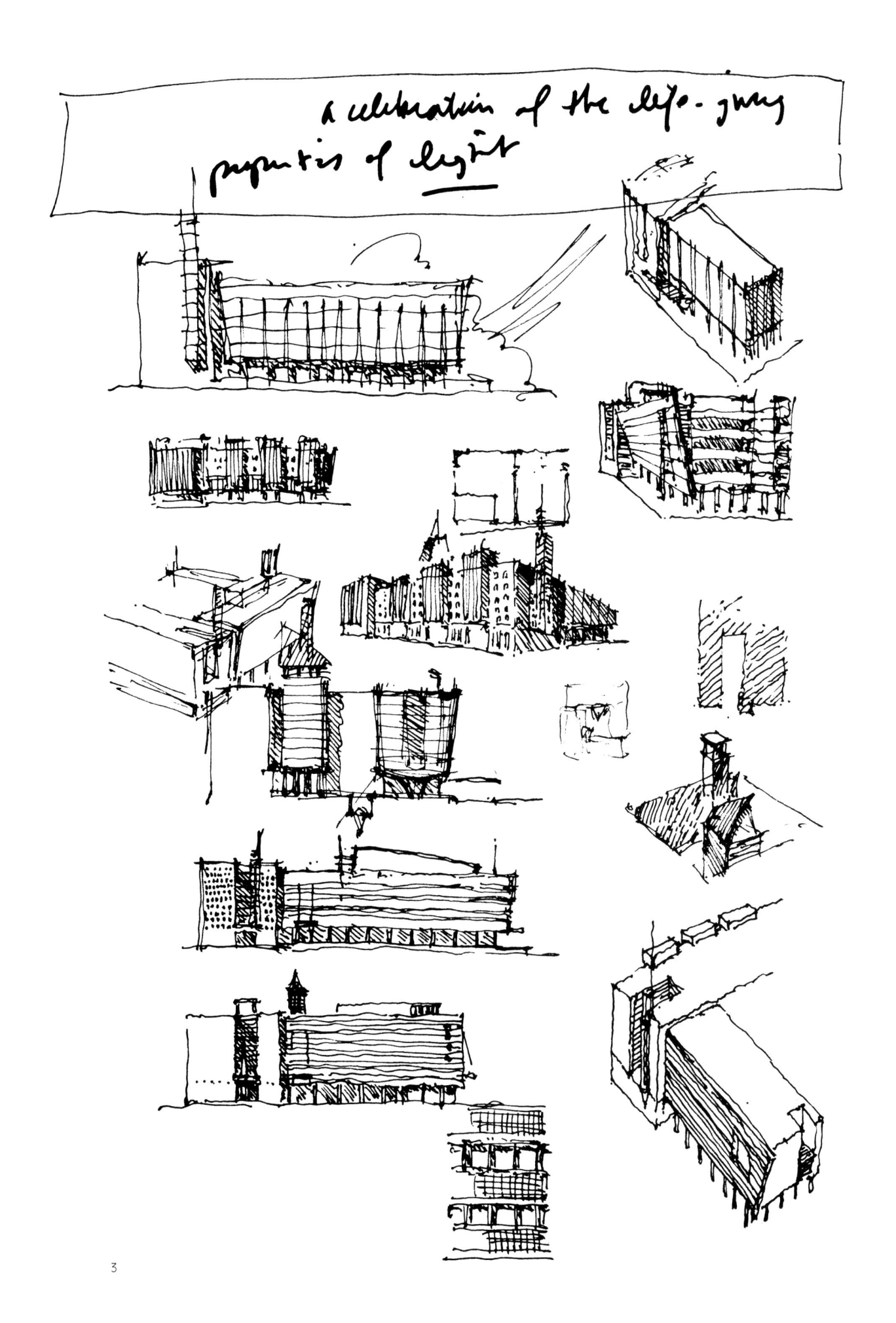

a celebration of the life-giving properties of light

First Competition Design

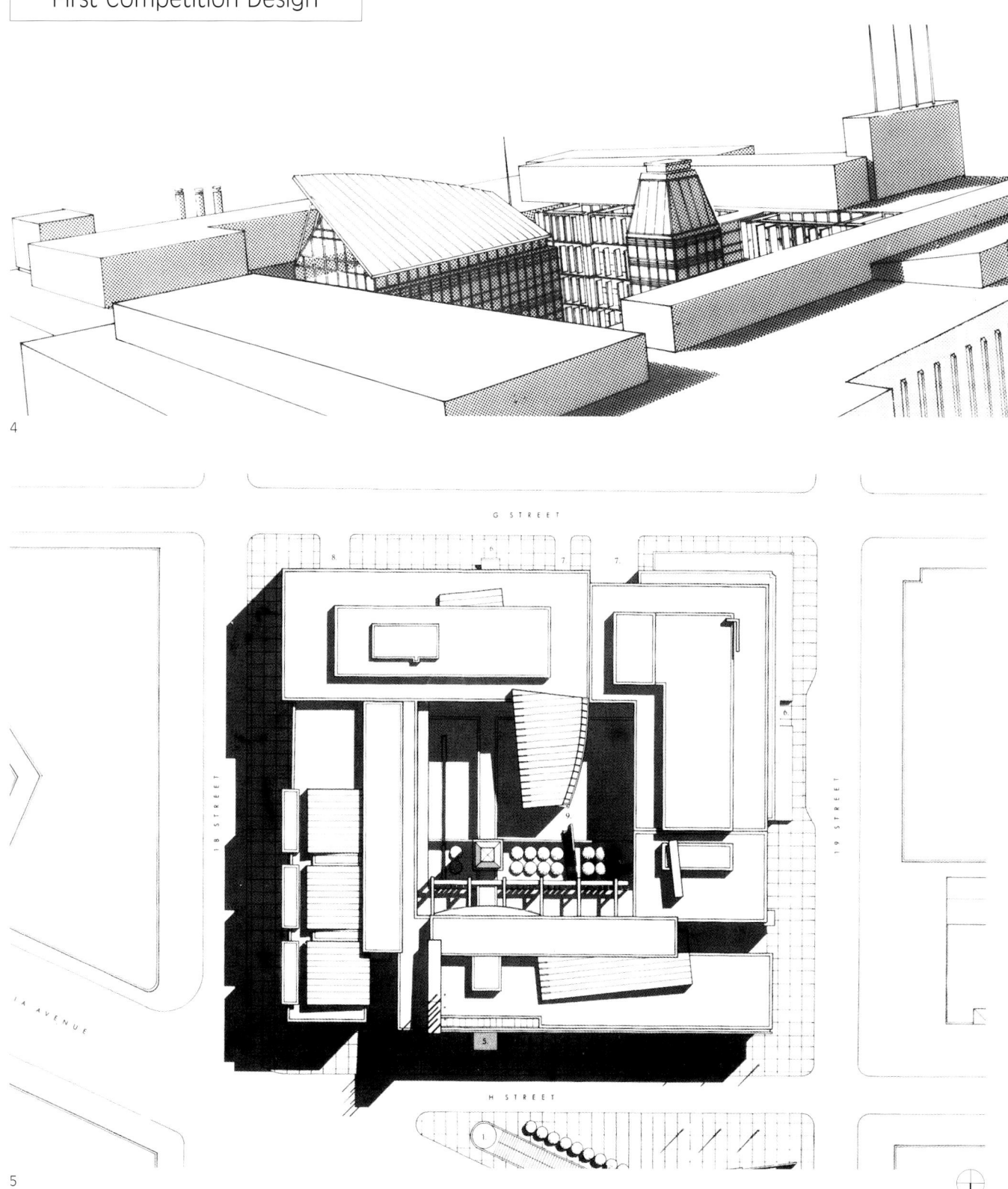

4

5

winner from the eight original submission, the panel inserted a second phase into the procedure, asking Skidmore, Owings & Merrill and Cannon, as well, for revised proposals in response to their comments and recommendations. It was at the evaluation panel's urging that KPF explored the possibility of a covered atrium – and came up with an improved design that won this final three-way contest.

The initial KPF design had shown two building wings projecting into the central open court. One, an office wing, was eliminated in the final scheme and its square footage redistributed to building volumes surrounding the atrium. The smaller projection of stacked conference rooms was retained as a vertical element inside the atrium.

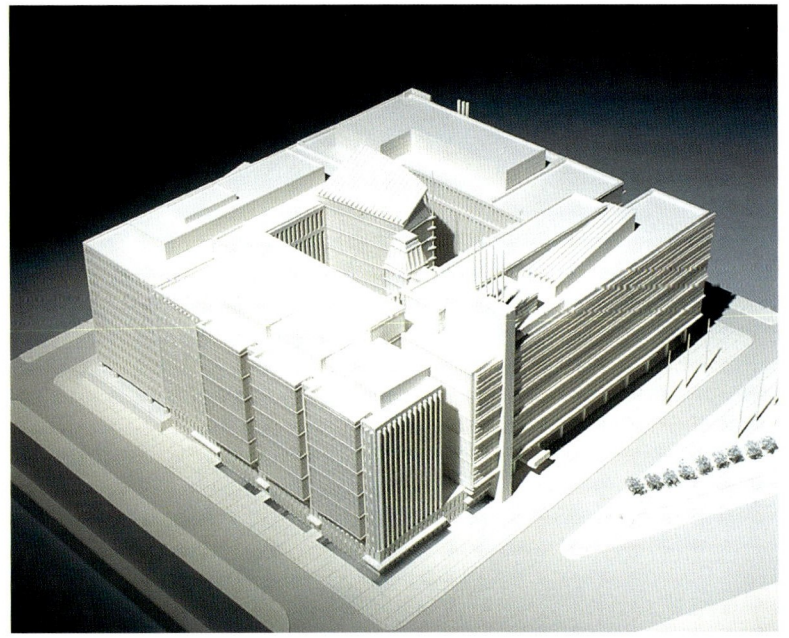

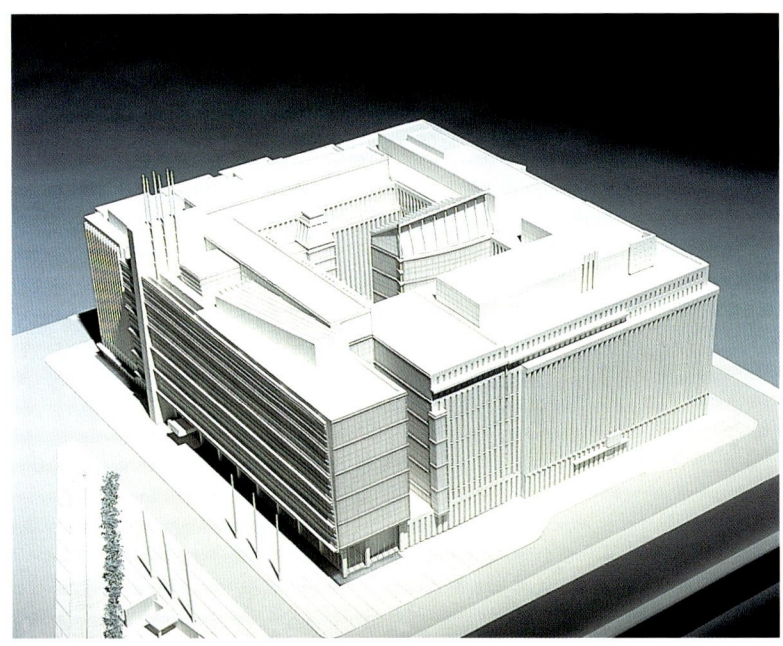

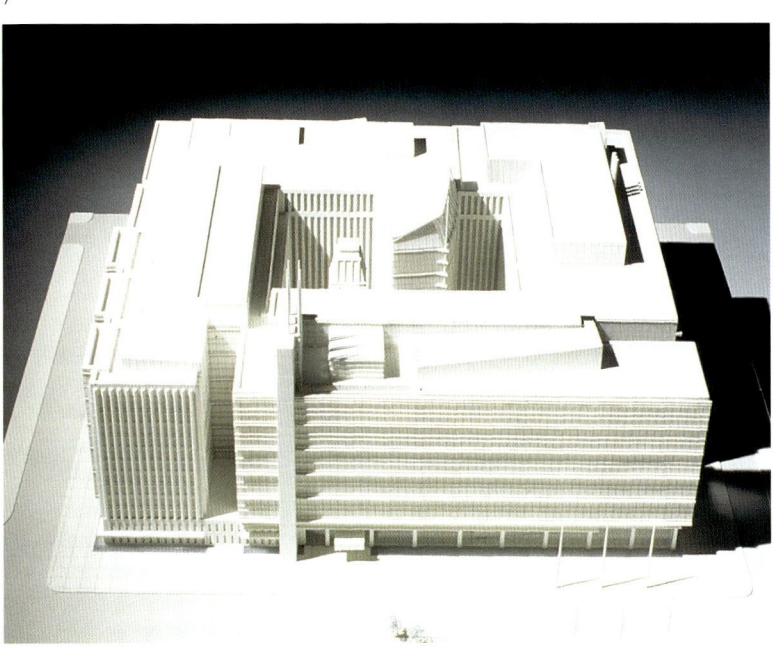

4 Rooftop perspective of first competition design.
5 Site plan of first competition design, showing open court at center.
6 Model of first competition design, viewed from northeast.
7 Model of first competition design, viewed from northwest.
8 Model of first competition design, viewed from north, showing main entrance façade.

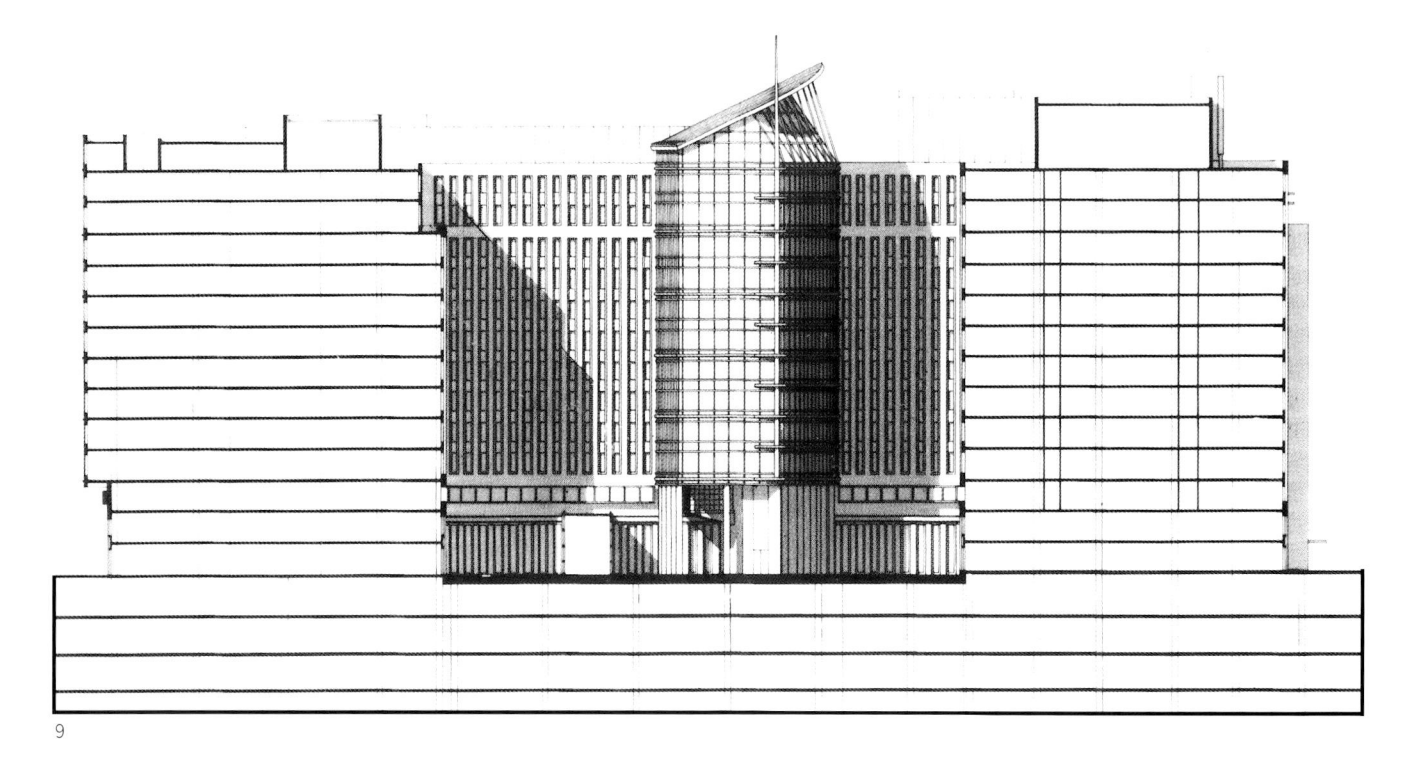

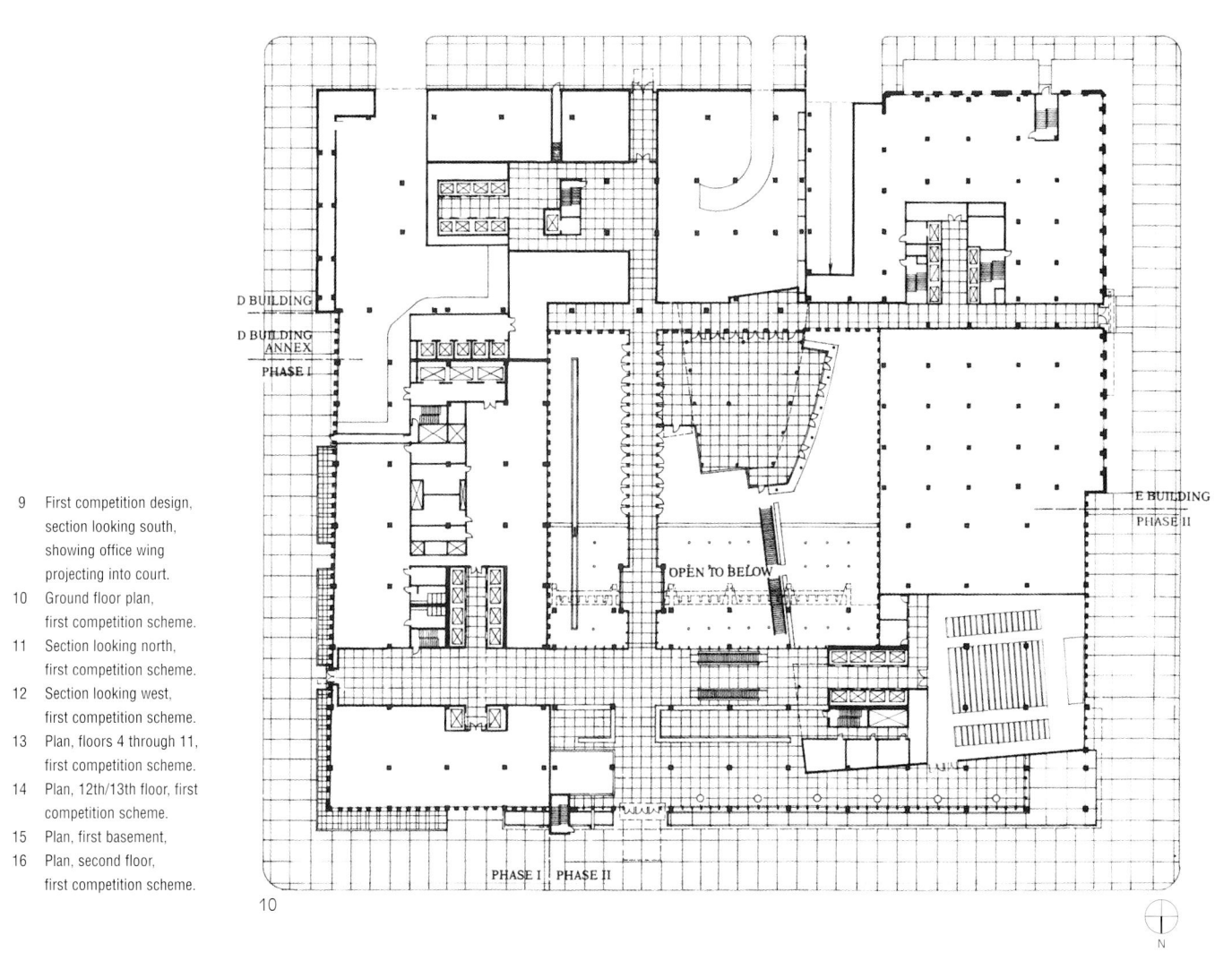

9 First competition design, section looking south, showing office wing projecting into court.
10 Ground floor plan, first competition scheme.
11 Section looking north, first competition scheme.
12 Section looking west, first competition scheme.
13 Plan, floors 4 through 11, first competition scheme.
14 Plan, 12th/13th floor, first competition scheme.
15 Plan, first basement,
16 Plan, second floor, first competition scheme.

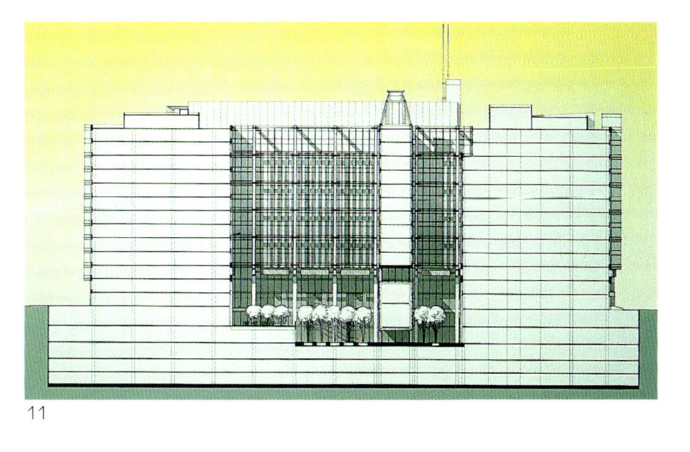

11

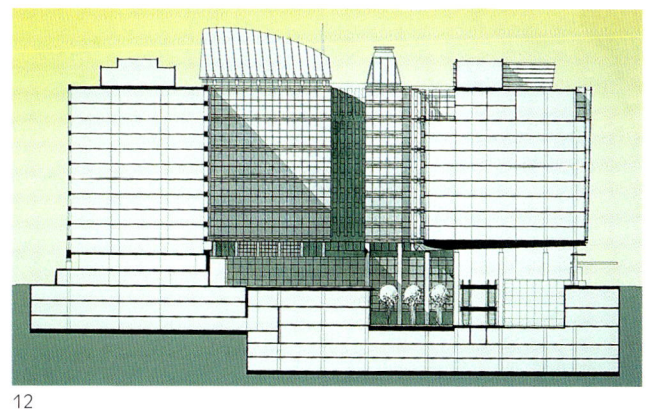

12

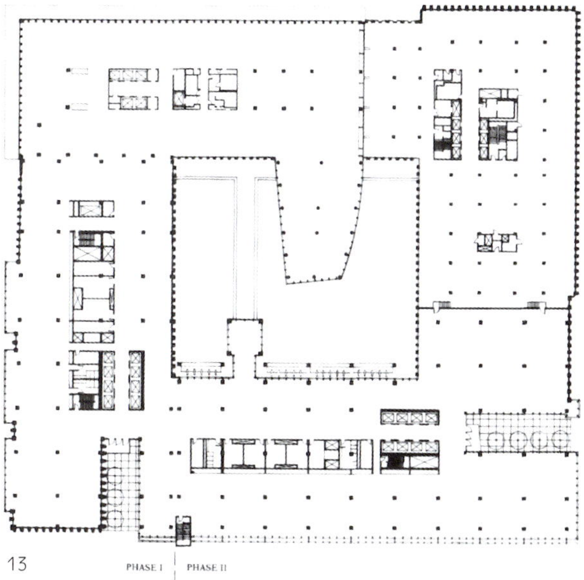

13 PHASE I | PHASE II

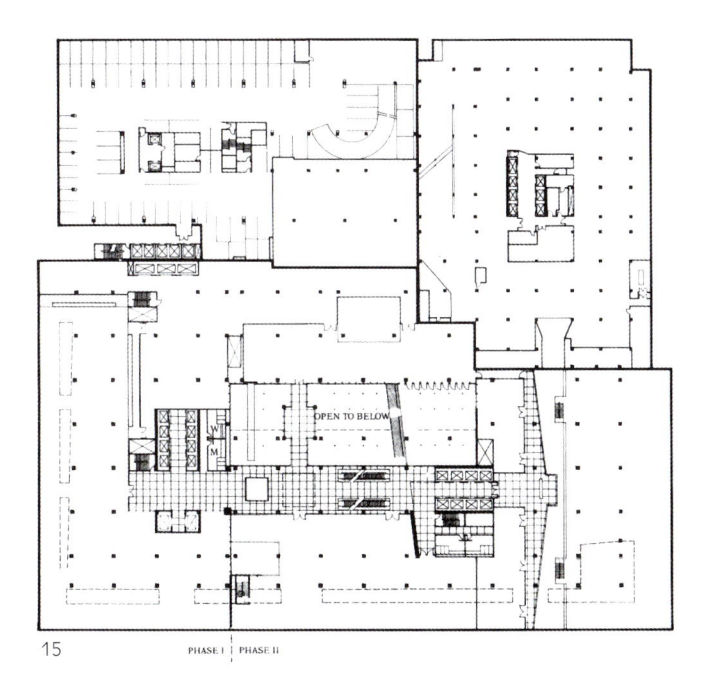

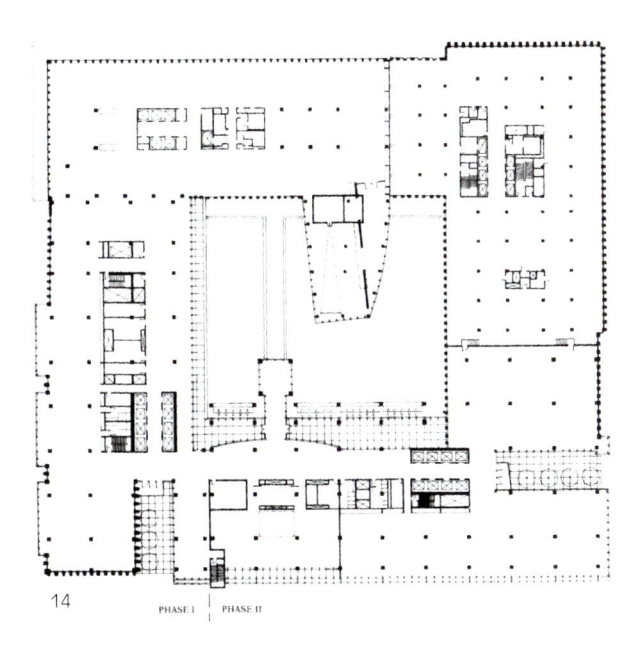

14 PHASE I | PHASE II

15 PHASE I | PHASE II

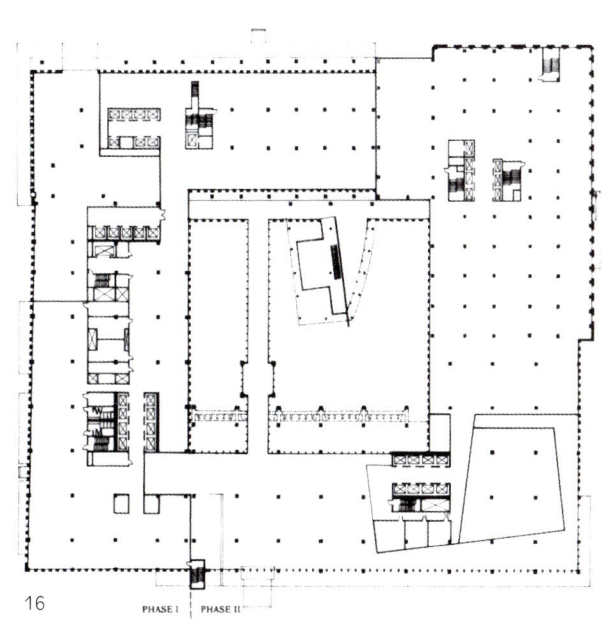

16 PHASE I | PHASE II

Covered atriums had occured in some of the other competing designs. (The design competition prospectus had suggested three small atriums to admit desired daylight.) But KPF's organization of the office volumes and the atrium is by far the clearest and easiest to comprehend: a 150-foot-square atrium (also, it happens, 150 feet high) at the center of the block, with a consistent band of office structures forming a square donut, in effect, around it.

One of the bank's needs was for relatively large amounts of exterior wall to provide windows for its numerous private offices and ample natural light to all employees' desks. The bank's work force is international, and they would not readily adjust to the vast unbroken office floors now common in America, where workers may be 50 or more feet from the nearest window. In KPF's plans for the new office floors here, floor spans are 52 feet 6 inches and, since a corridor runs down the center of these offices, no desk is farther than about 22 feet from a window wall. The division of the office floors by the notches that define the building's exterior volumes also helped extend the area of exterior wall. The success of the scheme with the people who work in the bank depended, of course, on their accepting offices facing the atrium as equivalent to exterior. And despite initial reservations, employees came to prize windows facing the atrium, which are not subjected to street noise or extremes of temperature and admit appealingly modulated daylight.

The container into which all these features so comfortably fit, the full-square-block exterior of the building, meets important symbolic and urbanistic objectives. In a neighborhood where most buildings of recent decades have presented some version of Washington's pervasive classical revival imagery, the World Bank offers a gust of fresh air. Its volumes appear relatively light and transparent, and they are made of manufactured materials.

From the bank's point of view, it was essential to avoid the Western classical tradition that is associated in the minds of many member countries with colonialism and to present an international image, rather than identify with the Washington's federal offices. KPF's design accomplishes this effectively, while nevertheless respecting its neighbors in terms of scale and color.

The contemporary character of this exterior was given a jump start by the decision to keep the two 1960's office blocks on the site, which present straightforward modernist exteriors from a period that resisted the city's pervasive classicism. With these as starting points, the architects developed harmonious designs for their new exterior walls. The completed exterior reads as an assemblage of different but closely related volumes, with the unique tilted glass plane of the block facing toward Pennsylvania Avenue—distinctive but not disruptive—clearly identified as the principal point of entry. If there is any doubt where to go in, the entrance canopy—low and simple, but suspended dramatically on long cables—makes it clear.

The few elements that project above the 130-foot line enliven the building's silhouette and identify its key spaces from a distance. The city's height regulations permit a small percentage of the building to exceed 130 feet, as long as this does not add occupied spaces— in other words, some top floor areas can have higher ceilings, in this case the Executive Directors' Conference Room and Board Room. Permission was also granted to raise the atrium roof to accommodate its curved long-span roof and admit additional light through clerestories.

Final Competition Design

17 Sketches proposing alternative wall treatment and rooftop elements for final competition design.

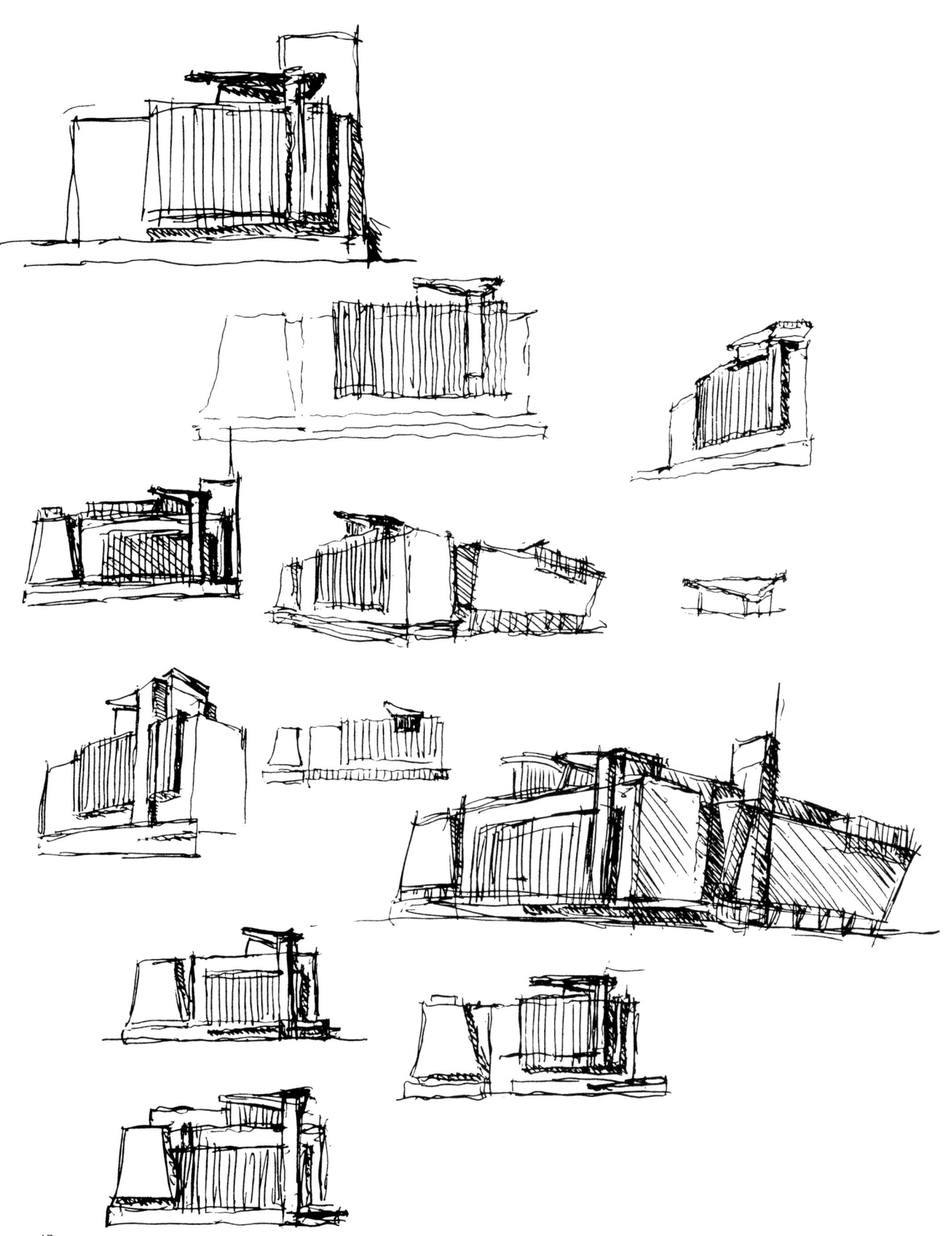

18

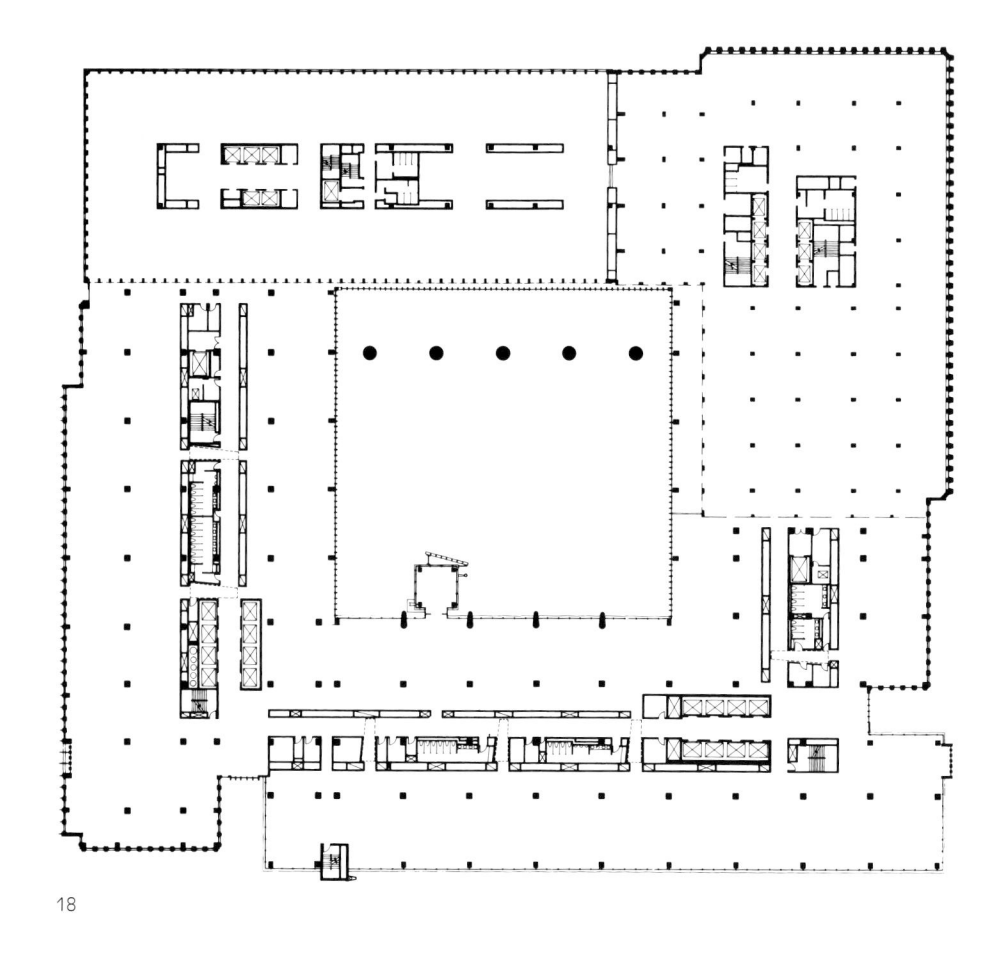

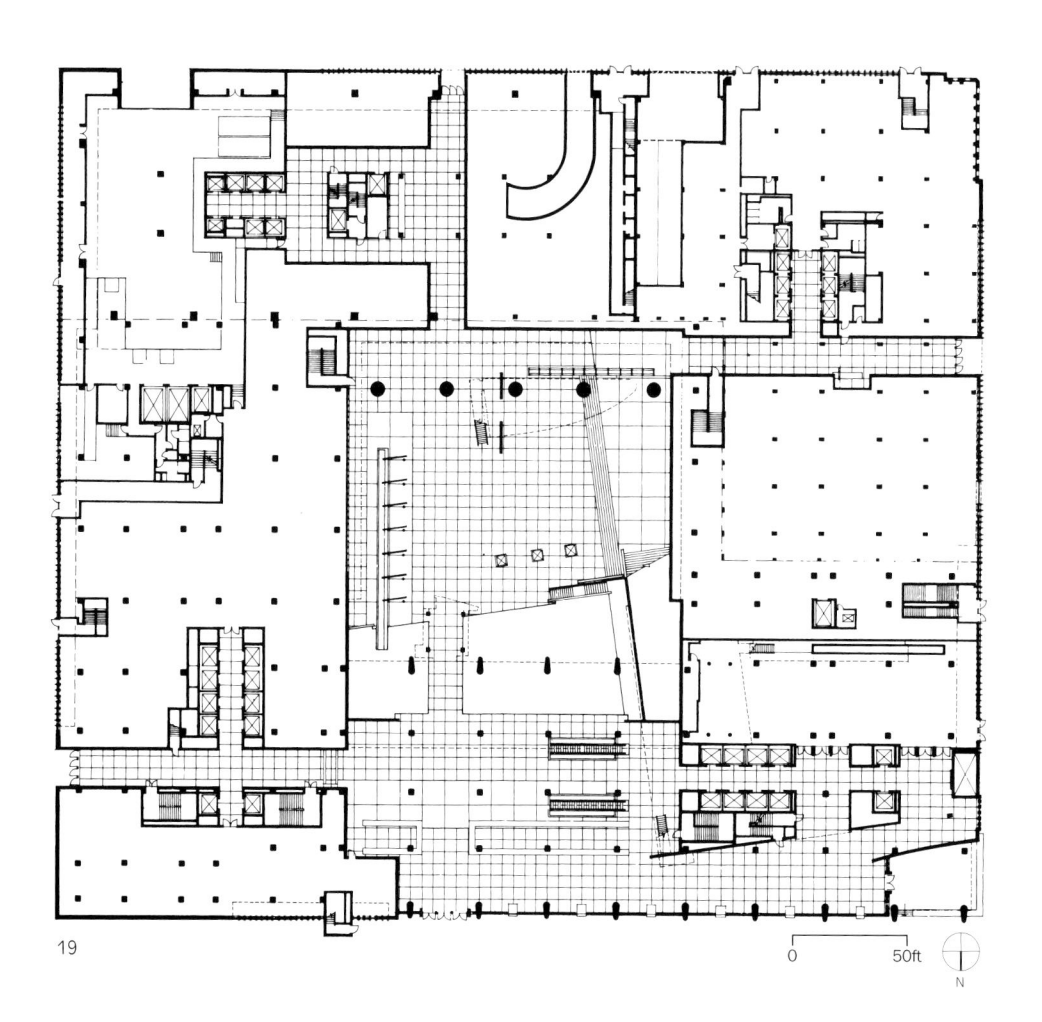

19

0 50ft

18 Typical floor plan
19 Ground floor plan
20 Roof plan
21 13th floor plan

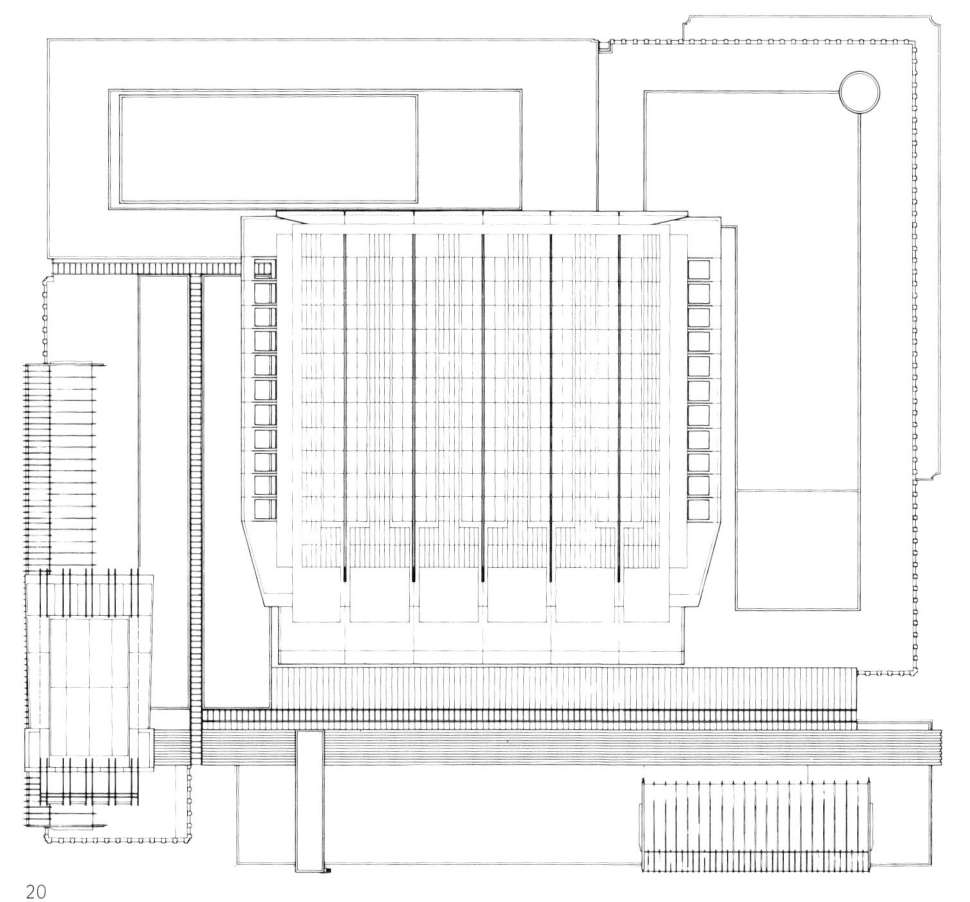

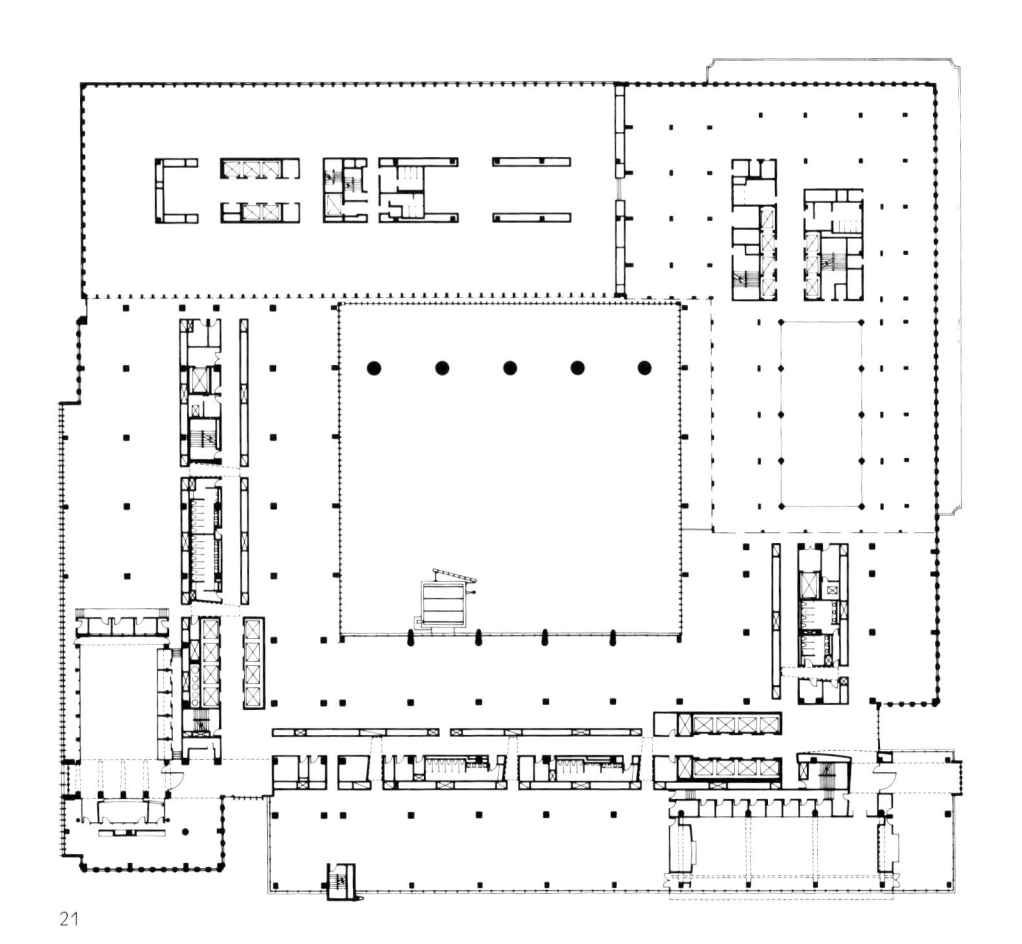

20

21

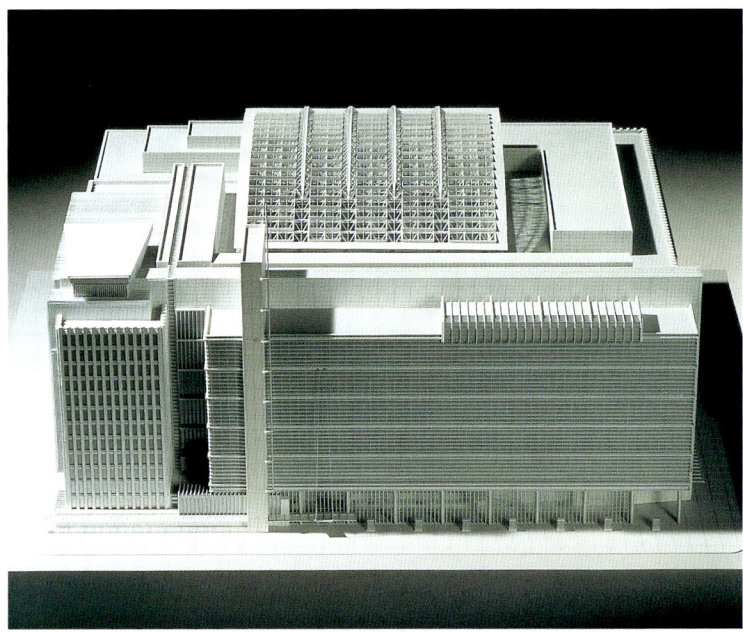

22 Final competition model viewed
    from northeast, Pennsylvania
    Avenue in foreground.
23 Final competition model viewed
    from north.
24 Final competition model viewed
    from northwest, small public
    park in foreground.
25 Final competition model viewed
    from northeast.
26 Final competition model viewed
    from north.
27 Final competition model viewed
    from northwest.

25

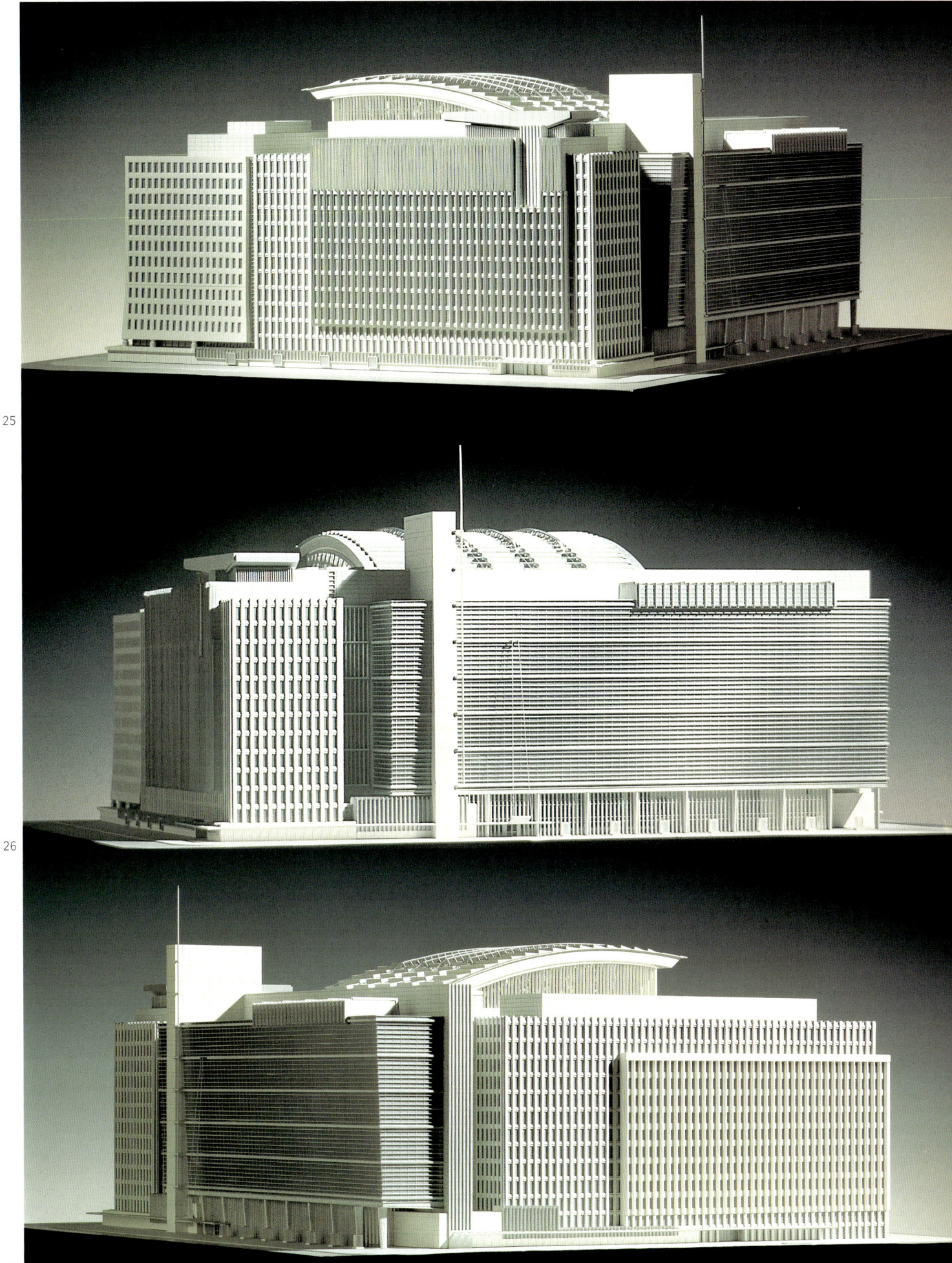

26

27

28 Final competition model viewed from northeast, showing Board Room penthouse with angular forms, rather than curved as actually built.

29 Final competition model, northwest corner, close to as-built design.

29

30

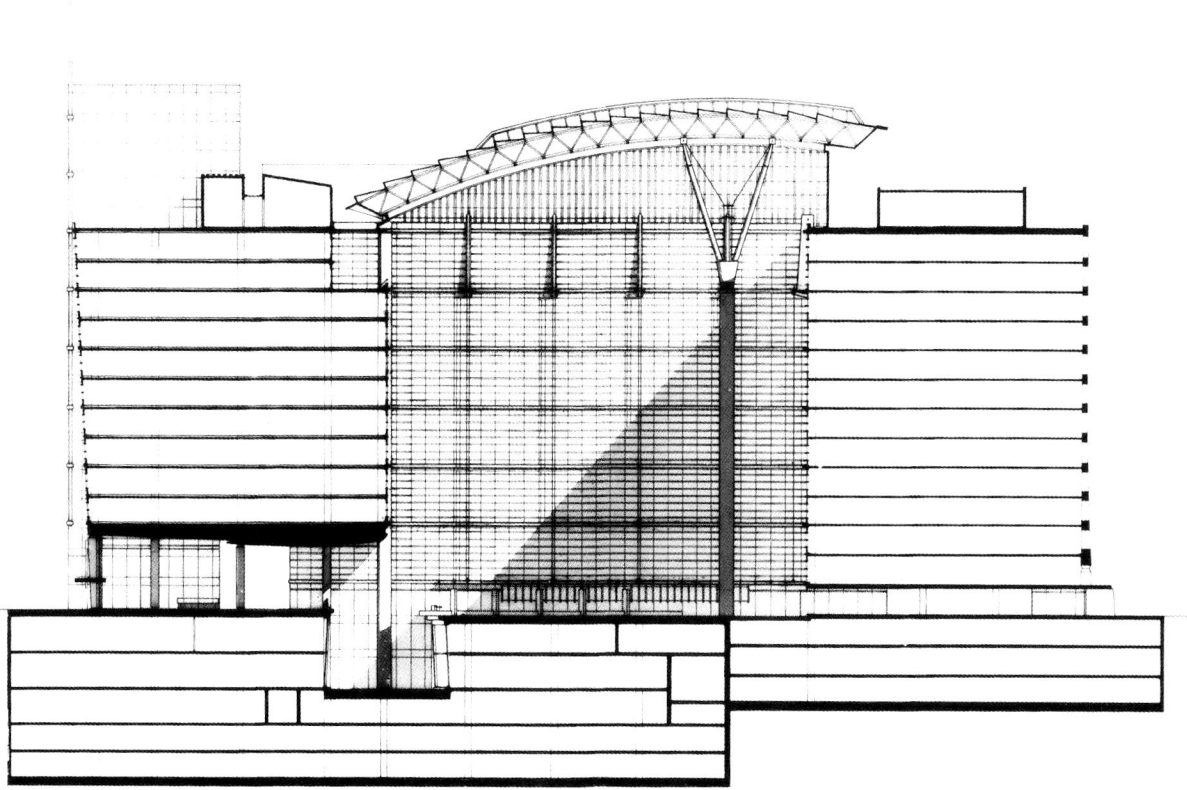

31

30 Atrium from central terrace, looking toward conference room tower.
31 Building section looking east.
32 Auditorium
33 Main lobby, at H Street entrance.

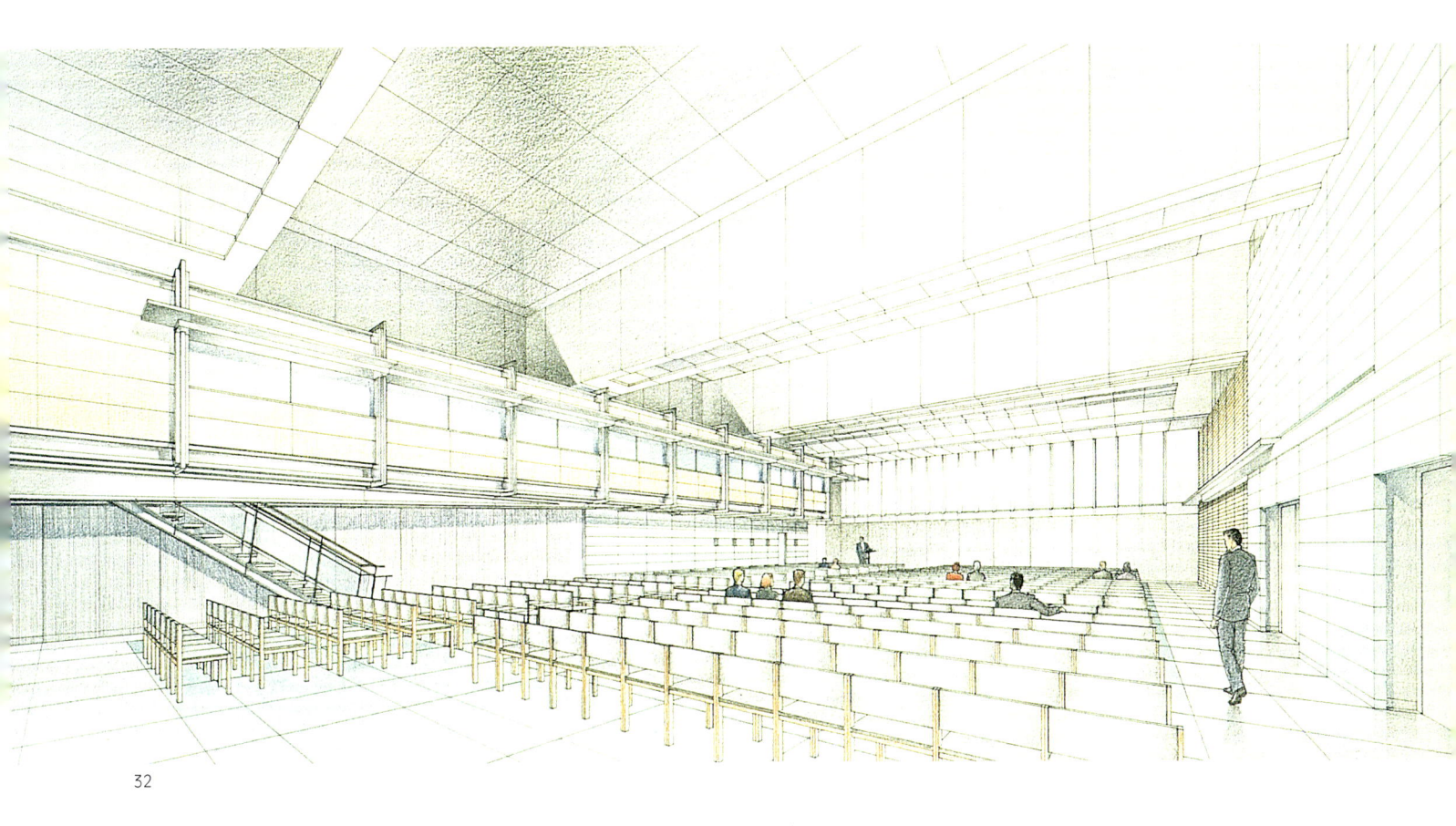

34

35

34 Reception hall from 1960s on upper floors of renovated E Building.
35 Executive Directors' Board Room.
Following pages:
　North front seen from across Pennsylvania Avenue.

45

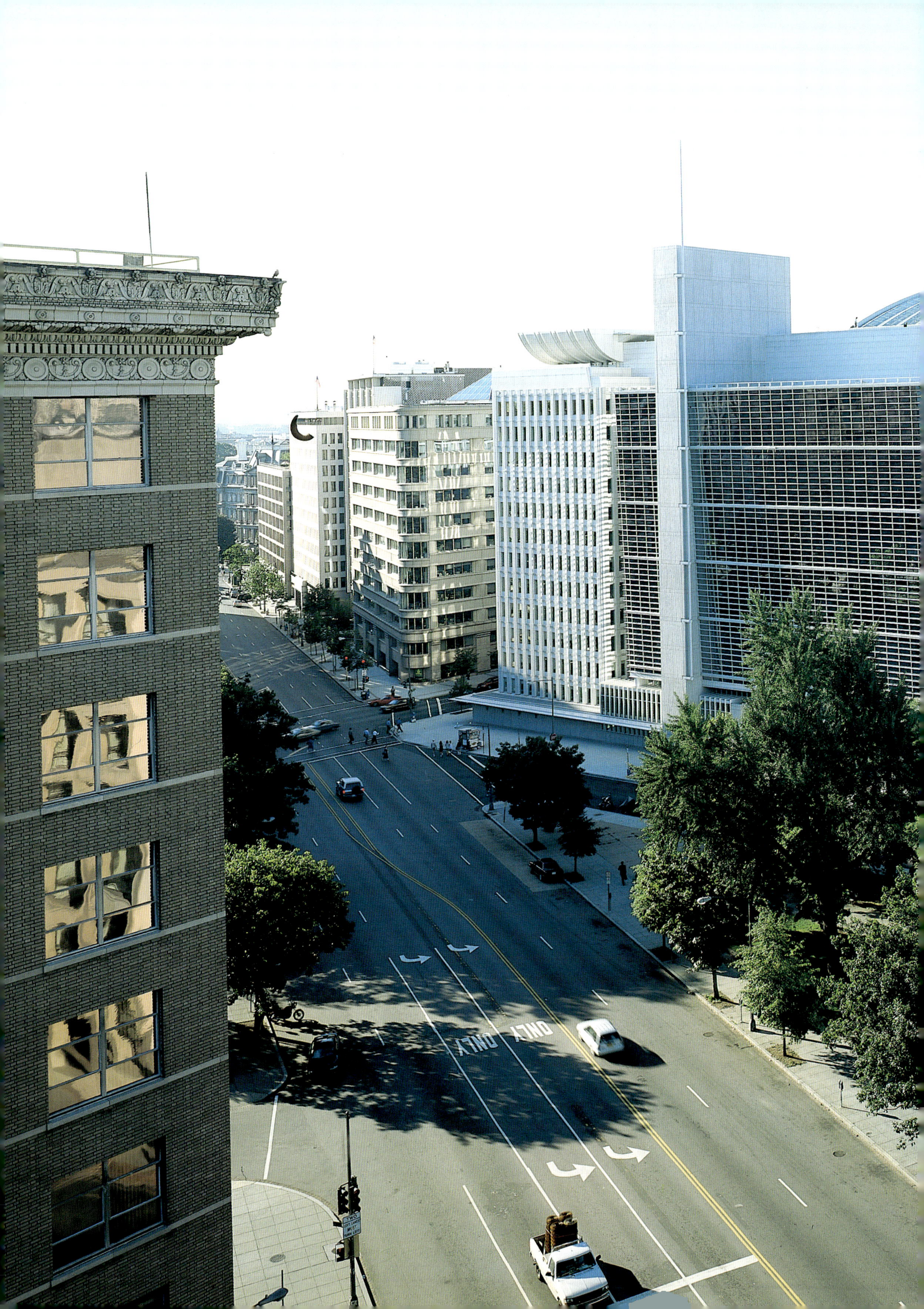

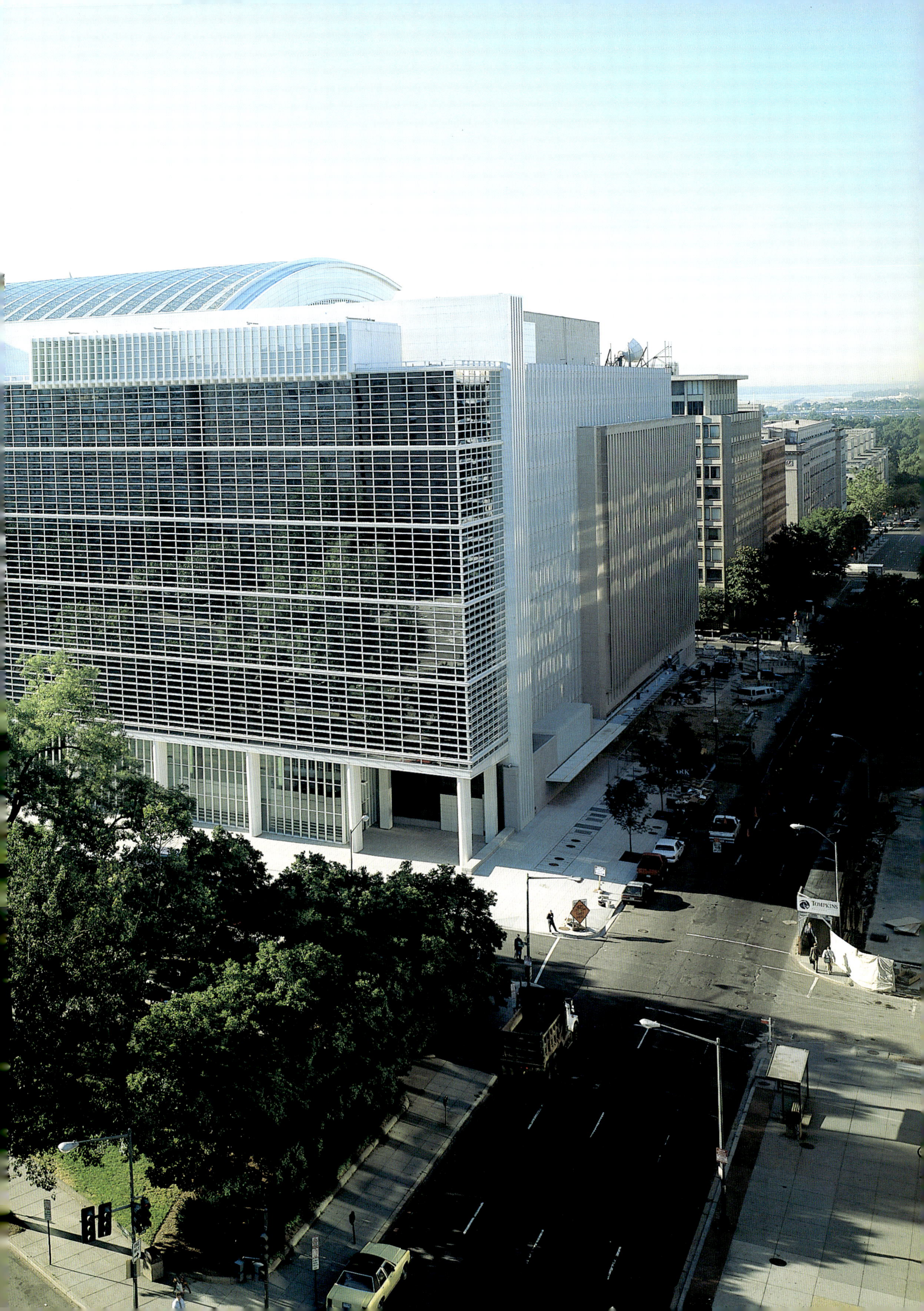
TOMPKINS

37 View from northwest, showing H Street front and 19th Street side.
38 View from northeast, showing 18th Street side and H Street front.

The finished World Bank building is remarkably faithful to the competition design, and staff members who worked with the architectural team credit that in large part to the design process. The bank deserves credit for developing a thorough and valid program, and KPF's final competition entry was painstakingly worked out, addressing the bank's every need in terms function and image. So very few adjustments were called for as the project moved on through construction. Of comparable importance in preserving the design intact was the process of selection by an impartial jury of experts and the full briefing that bank officials received during the competition. As is often the case with designs developed for well-run competitions, the endorsement of the scheme by both jury and client headed off virtually all the second-guessing that so often sends architects repeatedly back to the drawing board as projects proceed.

Once the competition-winning scheme was adopted, the architectural team was able to complete schematic design for this huge, complex building in only five months, largely because so much sound design work had already been done and accepted. After that, the most intense design effort went into refining the layout of the office areas. The design of systems for individual offices and workstations received the most detailed consideration.

A crucial consideration was the bank's virtually continuous changing of offices, as the organization is revamped and staff are reassigned within the building and rotated between this headquarters and field assignments all over the world. Offices with a high degree of standardization were developed to make possible a lot of shifting of personnel with minimal need for reconfiguring spaces. But assembling all offices from a small number of standard elements makes it possible to alter offices easily if necessary. Glazed clerestories in office partitions allow natural light to be dispersed throughout the floors and promote a feeling of openness.

Kohn Pedersen Fox's commission was unusually comprehensive, including most interiors. And while there was close cooperation with the bank's own facilities staff throughout, there was hardly any interference from higher levels of management. All in all, it was a rare opportunity for an architectural firm and the team it assembled to carry out a design down to the last detail.

STRUCTURAL/MECHANICAL SYSTEMS

The structural and mechanical systems of the World Bank are more than just technical devices to make the architectural concept work. They are integral components of the architectural concept.

It was by collaborating closely with the structural and mechanical engineers that the architects were able to develop one of the crucial virtues of their competition-winning design: the ability to fit 13 office floors in within the city's 130-foot height limit, which normally allows only 12.

Several interrelated structural and mechanical strategies made it possible to provide an 8-foot 1-inch ceiling height within a 10-foot 1¼-inch floor to-floor dimension, with 4½ inches given over to raised floors for power and communications. (The overall building height limits in Washington have made 8-foot office ceilings, considered low for offices in most cities, the expected standard.) One critical decision was the use of post-tensioned flat concrete slab floors, only 8 inches deep, rather than the customary 12 inches for conventional reinforced concrete. Because this concrete floor system was so advantageous, it was determined that the structural system throughout the office portions of the building would be concrete. High-strength concrete was used at selected locations to tailor column dimension to the needs of interior furniture system designs.

A second key design decision, in the area of mechanical engineering, was to reconsider the way air is distributed to office floors. Instead of the large ducts usually needed above the office ceilings to serve large areas, the system relies on frequently spaced vertical risers, along the centers of the office floors, from which unusually short ducts serve relatively small areas, thus making it possible to hold these horizontal ducts to a maximum depth of 6 inches (transitioning to 3 inches toward their ends, allowing perimeter offices an additional 3 inches of ceiling height). The vertical air ducts, along with the VAV air control boxes typically placed above the ceiling, are located in easily accessible closets along the central corridor of each office floor. Eliminating VAV boxes from the space above the ceiling also entailed providing perimeter offices with their own fan coil units along the outside walls.

Limited clearance above the ceilings ruled out recessed lighting fixtures and led to a system of indirect lighting, which is explained more fully in the pages on the typical office.

Accommodating power and communications services within a 4½-inch raised floor, with 3 inches clear under it, also required ingenuity. In order to provide adequate separation of telecommunications cables from electrical wiring, special trays were used for the cables, with closed bottoms where they pass over electrical lines and open ones elsewhere, allowing cables to be dropped out of the trays for distribution to workstations. This arrangement required electrical and

1

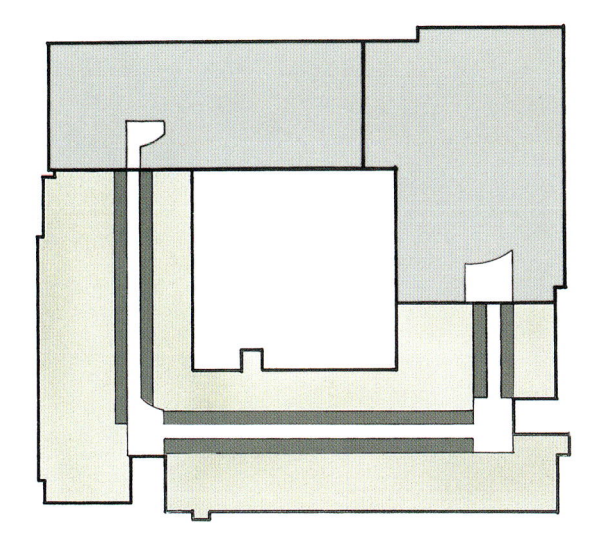

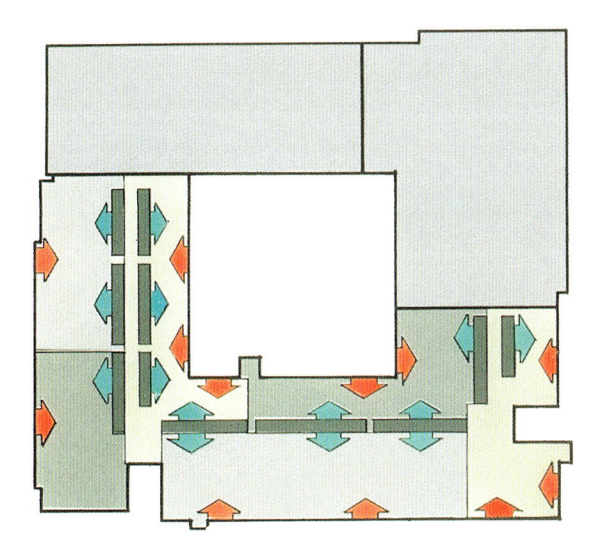

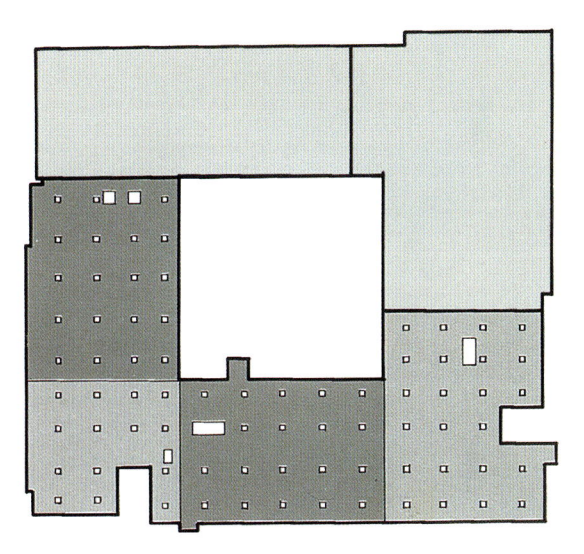

2

3

4

telecommunications engineers to draw up distribution grids at an early point in the design, so that the right configuration of cable trays could be installed to suit the two networks. The minimal dimensions under the raised floor even affected the construction tolerances for the pouring of the floor slabs, since a small deviation from specified dimensions could have caused major problems.

Having worked out a way to provide an extra story above ground, the structural engineers also found ways to build five much needed levels below grade, on a site where the high water table would ordinarily allow at most three levels. This was done by pouring slurry walls around the perimeter of the excavation, before

1   Plan of typical floor, showing linear cores which contain vertical air ducts and other services and also define central corridors through office areas.
2   Plan of typical floor, showing "neighborhood" divisions of office spaces sharing common services from linear cores.
3   Plan of typical floor, showing air distributed from linear cores and perimeter units and zones for controlling air, which can be further adjusted at individual workstations.
4   Plan of typical floor, showing distribution of electrical and communications systems, extending from central closets to bay boxes and connecting to raceways in partitions.

5 6 7 8

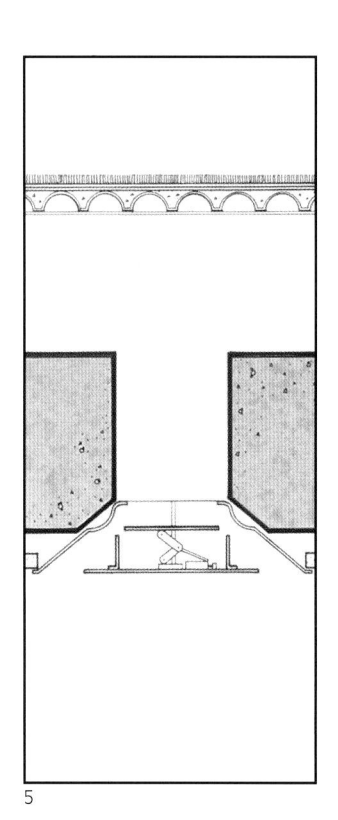

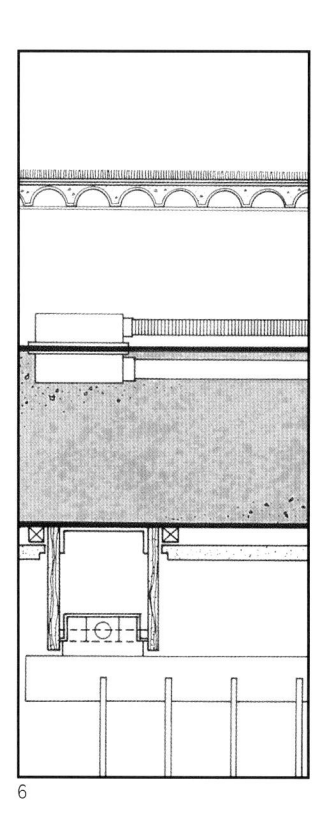

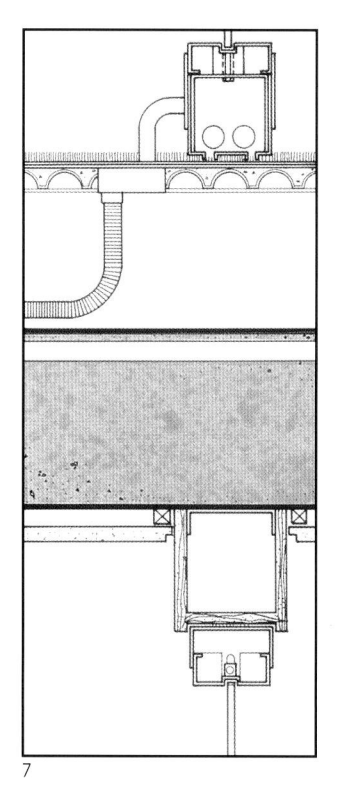

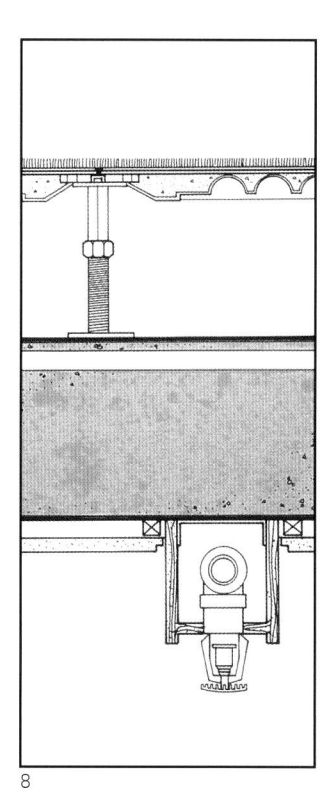

constructing a foundation with a 3-foot-deep concrete mat at the bottom, thickened to 5 feet under the bases of columns and some other areas to counteract the uplift effect of hydrostatic pressures. The 30-inch permanent foundation walls carry part of the structural load of the five basement levels, the ground floor superstructure, and the perimeter columns.

The atrium roof presented a distinct structural challenge of its own. It was not possible to impose any of its additional load on the older buildings that bound it on two sides, and this limitation inspired a support system that eloquently expresses its structural rationale. Along the north side of the atrium, the roof is firmly attached to the courtyard walls of the new Phases One and Two buildings, which are designed to take the lateral component of the roof load, as well as the vertical. Supporting the south side of the roof is a line of 126-foot-tall columns, set 28 feet away from the wall of the existing D Building.

Concrete was chosen for the columns in part for consistency with the rest of the building, in part because steel would have been more expensive. Each of the 5-foot-diameter columns is topped by an inverted tubular steel assemblage, its arms accepting the space frame at its nodes. Visually, the domain of concrete construction, up to approximately the prevailing roof level, is clearly separated from the domain of lighter steel

ELECTRICAL CONDUIT BELOW
SOLID BOTTOM TRAY SEGMENT

ACCESS FLOOR

SOLID BOTTOM TRAY
SEGMENT 12' LONG (366cm)

ELECTRICAL JUNCTION BOX

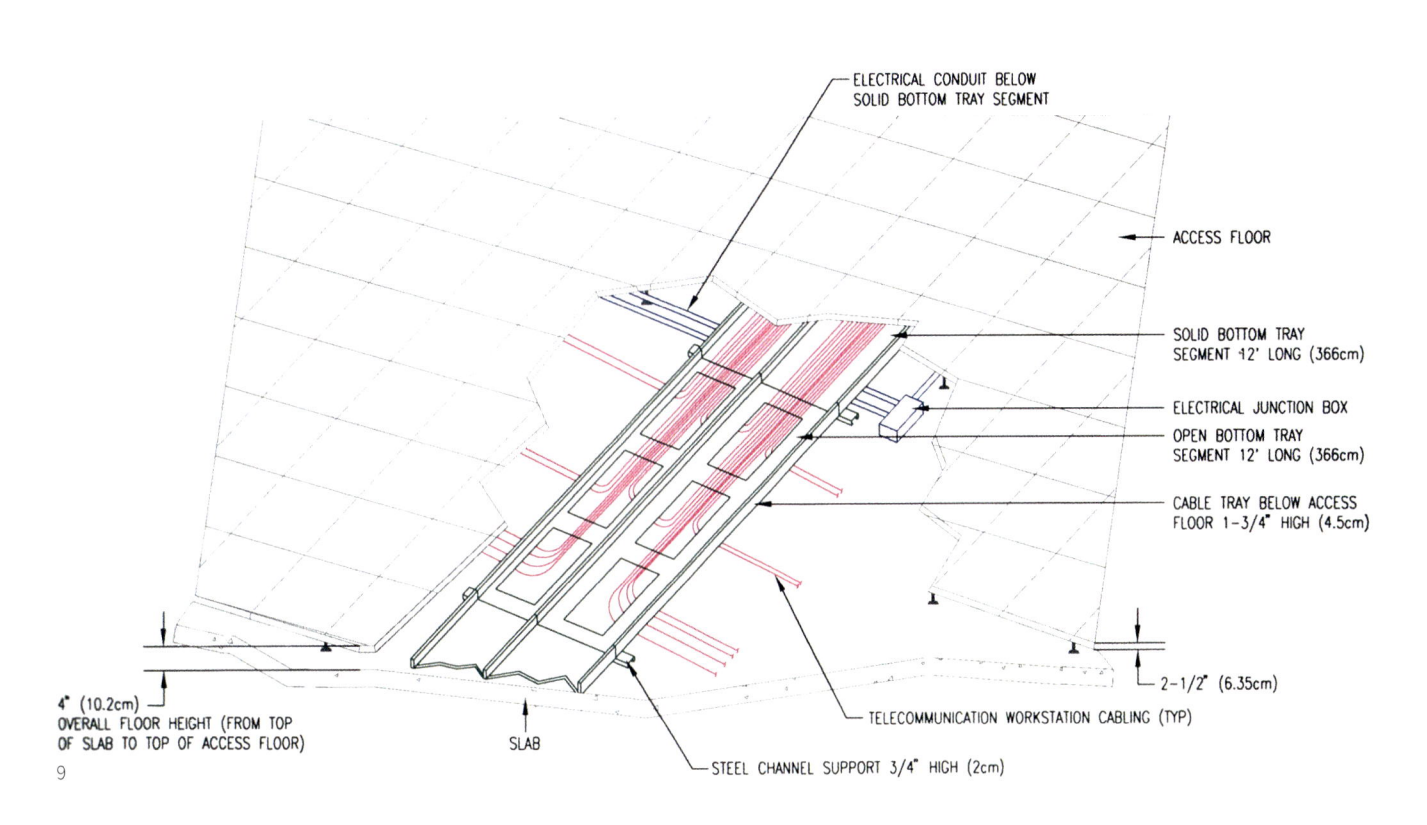

OPEN BOTTOM TRAY
SEGMENT 12' LONG (366cm)

CABLE TRAY BELOW ACCESS
FLOOR 1-3/4" HIGH (4.5cm)

2-1/2" (6.35cm)

TELECOMMUNICATION WORKSTATION CABLING (TYP)

STEEL CHANNEL SUPPORT 3/4" HIGH (2cm)

4" (10.2cm)
OVERALL FLOOR HEIGHT (FROM TOP
OF SLAB TO TOP OF ACCESS FLOOR)

SLAB

9

construction for the atrium roof. Instead of the columns providing lateral support for the space frame, the space frame provides lateral support for the columns.

The space-frame itself arcs up to a high point 45 feet above the surrounding 130-foot roof level (the city's height limitations allowing for some upward extensions of spaces below, such as domes). The tubular components of the space-frame roof vary in both exterior diameter and wall thickness, depending on their different loads at different locations, but they look consistent except under careful scrutiny.

On the three sides of the atrium roof that are not supported by adjacent office wings, a clerestory curtain wall between the atrium roof and the building roofs is held in place with sliding Teflon steel connections, which allow for dimensional changes in the 150-foot-square roof under various thermal, gravity, and lateral forces, as well as differential movement of the four structures around it.

5   Section drawing showing pressurized raised floor supplying air to individually thermostatically controlled air diffusers for offices below.
6   Section showing bay boxes supplying power to office workstations, with lighting for floor below spanning between ceiling-mounted junction boxes.
7   Section showing modular demountable partition system that allows for simple rearrangement of offices and workstations.
8   Section showing sprinklers and piping enclosed within modular grid.
9   Schematic drawing of electrical and communications systems below raised floor.

CONSTRUCTION PROCESS

1

2

Construction of the new headquarters took place in three phases, so that the bank could occupy offices on most of the site throughout the process. New construction was carried out in two phases, with a third phase for retrofitting the two existing buildings incorporated into the complex.

The actual phasing of new construction did not quite correspond to the visible volumes of the finished building. Phase one construction included a short portion of the entrance block facing H Street, with its distinctive tilted glass façade. The actual joint between construction phases is marked by the stair tower near the main entrance. One of its purposes is separating two areas of the same curtain wall, erected about two years apart, which could not be expected to match in color because of weathering. On the west (19th Street) side of the complex, there is a similar disparity between apparent building volumes and actual construction, with much of the new phase two structure clad in curtain wall that suggests it is an extension of the existing E Building.

The foundations of the complex were built to make possible five levels below grade despite the high water table and attendant hydrostatic pressures. Excavations reached 23 feet below the site's water table. The slurry trench method was used to build the 30-inch-thick foundation walls, constructed with five levels of tie-backs that extended below surrounding streets and

3

buildings—the upper ones anchored in soil, the lower ones to rock. These tie-backs were released as basement floors were completed, acting as diaphragms to brace the foundation walls from inside. Phase one started with a 120 feet by 270 feet by 60-foot-deep excavation. Phase two required an L-shaped excavation, 120 feet by 270 feet by 300 feet, 60 feet deep.

A mud slab was poured at the bottom of each excavation, and reinforcing for the actual slab assembled on that. This bottom slab is 3 feet thick, increasing to 5 feet under columns and at the bases of elevator banks. The slab at the base of the each excavation was also constructed with designated locations for tower cranes, which were used to construct the floor slabs that rose around them. As construction proceeded above ground, each floor required the complex installation of cables for the post-tensioning that was critical to the thin-slab structural system.

In order to establish a level of craftsmanship for the building's architectural concrete, construction teams were required to visit the East Building of the National Gallery, about a mile from the site, to examine the cast-in-place concrete there. KPF partner William Pedersen had worked on that museum in the early 1970s, as a designer in the office of I.M. Pei & Partners. Joseph P. Ruocco, who represented KPF at the bank's building site, conferred on

1   Demolition of B & C Buildings and partial demolition of A Building makes way for Phase 1 construction.

2   Demolition for Phase 1 nears completion, with SOM's D Building exposed in background.

3   Excavation for five underground levels reaches about 25 feet below site's water table. Need for five basements was driven by competition program, which called for two levels of parking and a large printing facility, among other underground spaces. Slurry walls 30-inch-thick form vertical foundation walls, with horizontal pockets ready to accept horizontal slabs of subsurface floors.

4

5

concrete quality with the retired project manager for Tompkins Construction on the museum project.

Under the bank's fast-track construction process, the foundation walls around the excavations were started before the final column locations had been determined. Subsequently, the column locations were fixed before the plans for all floors were completed. While columns were being cast on the lower floors above grade, the columns at the 13th-floor Executive Directors' Board Room had to be changed in their dimensions to accommodate the room's layout around the custom table specified as its principal focus.

The fast-track procedure affected the design of the supports for the curtain wall at the edge of the above-grade floor slabs. Since curtain wall contractors had not yet bid on the walls when the slabs were being completed, continuous galvanized plates were installed at the slab edges, so that walls could be connected at any point. Thus curtain wall contractors were free to price out a variety of unitized or stick-built systems for constructing the walls and arrive at the most favorable competitive pricing.

Phase two construction included not only one of the principal office blocks along H Street, but the atrium that forms the core of the complex. Part of the phase two construction involved

4 Undergoing constant de-watering, excavation for Phase 1 requires 3-inch-thick mud slab of concrete atop bentonite panel.
5 Once mud slab has cured, column foundation reinforcement is installed.
6 Parking garage shuttle elevator foundation begins to take shape.
7 Foundation mat reinforcing, with thickened mat in 5-foot-deep columns and deeper depressions for elevator cores and pits.

extending the east side of the E Building 13 feet, bringing it out to form one wall of the new atrium and providing space for a line of private offices overlooking it.

Construction of the 150-foot-square atrium roof was a challenge quite distinct from that of the office blocks. Casting the five concrete columns that support the south side of the roof to appear uniform their entire height was one of the difficult requirements. The columns are made of board-formed concrete poured in six 20-foot lifts. The construction crew started working on the problem a year in advance, using mock-ups, to get the concrete mix and the custom formwork just right.

Erecting the spaceframe roof on these columns presented another series of challenges. Connecting the columns to the spaceframe itself are 40-foot-high, four-branched assemblies composed of 14-inch-diameter steel tube, which had to be hoisted from the atrium floor to the tops of the concrete shafts. Since the roof was put in place in the heat of a Washington summer, the sun shining on the concrete columns could cause one side to expand, distorting them out of correct alignment. So the shafts had to be temporarily stayed with cables to keep them in position.

8 Steel reinforcing for slab is installed. Slurry wall in background jogs around existing tunnel connecting D Building to J Building below intervening street.
9 Shoring for basement slabs is installed around two tower cranes used for construction of Phase 1.
10 Workers tie steel reinforcing rods.
11 Reinforcing is installed for first level of basement.
12 Close-up of Phase 1 framing shows risers for perimeter fan coil air conditioning units located between column faces and edges of slabs. Galvanized steel plates anchored to slab edges reflect fast-track schedule by facilitating connection of curtain wall at any possible point, thus allowing competitive bidding by contractors proposing various wall assembly methods.
13 Two-story precast concrete piers of curtain wall are installed on upper floors.
14 Framing of Phase 1 reveals cantilever of slabs for 4th through 13th floor for 7-foot-6-inch projection along 18th Street.
15 Exterior cladding of Phase 1 structure is almost completed, and Board Room framing rises above main roof level.

12

13

14

15

16

17

18

The spaceframe roof was then erected, supported along the north side by a phase two office block and, 120 feet to the south, on the five columns. The 32,400-square-foot spaceframe was detailed to absorb the dynamic movements of the five separate foundation systems that support it.

Control of rainwater runoff from the atrium roof also required special attention. The city's stormwater management required the roofs to retain 3 inches of standing water. The volume of water shed by the atrium roof resulted in a 7-inch depth on the roofs. The valleys of the rooftop skylight were designed as sluices to direct the water onto adjoining roofs, principally the roof of the phase two block along H Street. During an exceptional thunderstorm near completion of the project, the design team discovered that the water was shed by the skylight with such volume and speed that it jumped a 12-foot gap to enter air intake louvers in a penthouse wall. The architects, along with their fountain consultant, designed a series of metal baffles to break up such a water flow before it reached the louvers.

From the beginning of planning for the design competition, the bank made a point of organizing the process so that no employees would have to move more than twice during the years of construction, and many would move only once. Administering the personnel moves for some 4,700 people, in a block-square building where no part remained habitable throughout the entire process, was a major logistical effort that went on simultaneously with the construction.

16 Phase 1 construction is seen from Pennsylvania Avenue, with precast curtain wall partially installed. Portions of existing World Bank buildings along H Street remain in use.
17 Phase 1 construction is essentially finished, including one bay of metal and glass curtain wall that will later expand across H Street front.
18 Phase 1 in final stages of construction, is seen from 18th Street side. Note four distinct types of curtain walls on that side and first bay of angular wall on H Street front.
19 On G Street front, existing E Building at left is linked to existing D Building at right by new construction with precast curtain wall, plus narrow vertical "zipper wall" at edge of D Building.
20 Band of new construction extends E Building 13 feet, with new curtain wall facing what will become central atrium.
21 Portion of Phase 2 construction is viewed from 19th Street. Various types of metal and glass curtain wall enclose projection to left and recessed portion at center. Precast wall at right makes transition to E Building farther along street.
22 View from Pennsylvania Avenue shows complex after demolition of remaining portion of A Building, plus F Building, ready for Phase 2 construction.

23

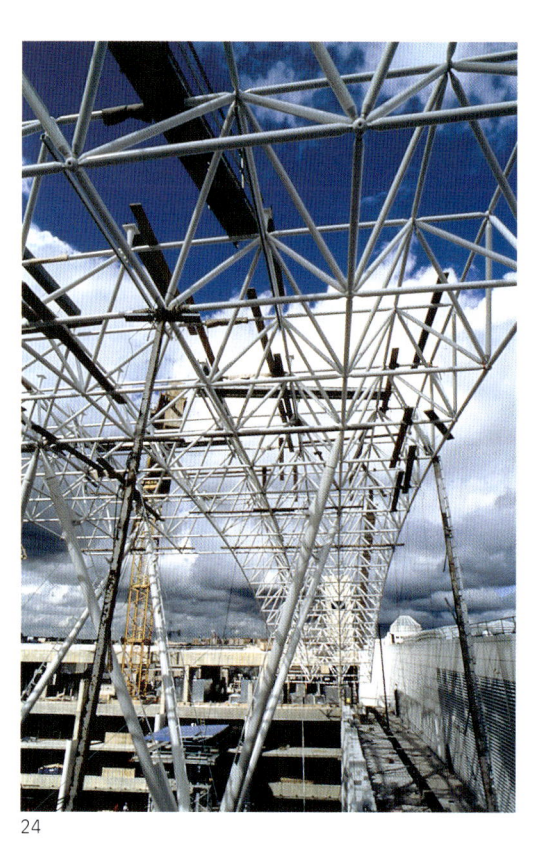

24

25

26

23 Erecting space frame roof of atrium in sections was most demanding construction challenge. Because thermal effects of summer sun could distort 126-foot-high cylindrical columns (at right), they had to be stayed temporarily with cables before the space frame was put in place to brace them.
24 Progress photo shows first band of space frame in place.
25 Atrium skylight roof, seen nearing completion, required special measures to control flow of heavy rainfall into the city drainage system at acceptable rate. To limit flow, adjoining roofs had to be designed to accept 7-inch depth of water in storms.
26 The space frame of atrium roof spans 120 feet from centerlines of tree-like tops of five cylindrical columns (foreground) to the wall of Phase 2 building (background). Covering 32,500 square feet, space frame is designed to absorb the movements of five separate foundation systems that support it.
27 Steel members carry space frame load to tops of 5-foot-diameter concrete columns.
28 View from atrium floor shows entire space frame in place.

27

28

BUILDING ENVELOPE

Evolution of KPF Curtain Walls

The curtain wall treatment of the World Bank exemplifies an approach to the building envelope that has evolved through a series of projects by Kohn Pedersen Fox Associates. Several key buildings designed in the few years before World Bank show variations in curtain wall design visually breaking down the overall building mass into discreet volumes. In the five projects illustrated here, differences in wall treatment distinguish portions of the buildings that differ in function, relate low- or medium-rise blocks at the bases of buildings to their urban neighbors, and reduce the apparent mass of high-rise portions by expressing them as clusters of towers or thin slabs. At the World Bank, similar design strategies were applied to assimilate two existing buildings as elements in a full-city-block assemblage of visually distinct volumes.

1 Rockefeller Plaza West, New York, New York
2 The St. Paul Companies Headquarters, St. Paul, Minnesota
3 Westendstrasse 1 DG Bank Headquarters, Frankfurt, Germany
4 1250 Boulevard Rene-Levesque, Montreal, Canada
5 Federal Reserve Bank of Dallas, Dallas, Texas

3

4

5

Design of World Bank Curtain Walls

The design of the World Bank curtain walls is critical in conveying the architects' concept of a series of related volumes, set in a pinwheel pattern around the perimeter of its city block. The four fronts of the building are distinguished by four dominant volumes (two existing, two new), each visibly holding one of the corners of the block and extending along one front. The faces of the two new blocks in this assemblage are subdivided so each single expanse of wall is roughly in the scale of the existing structures.

The great tilted plane of the entry front is subtly designed to be the most prominent face of the bank and to enhance its urban setting. By tilting forward at 3 degrees, it gracefully announces both its distinction (its object-like quality) among the other volumes of the bank as the main entry front. And the tilt also makes it more effective as a containing wall for the small square along Pennsylvania Avenue—a green patch that needs reinforcing so it is not lost in the sweep of surrounding streets. The wisdom of breaking up each block front with visually different wall surfaces is apparent if you imagine this tilted plane extended the entire length of the block: it would be an overbearing presence in relation to the park and to neighboring buildings, and its connection to the rest of the headquarters complex would be broken.

The other distinguishing characteristic of the H Street block is its pattern of horizontal members, within larger two-story-high bands. Reiterated in an external grid (referred to in building-team shorthand as "monkey-bars") the grid develops a rich, layered pattern of rectangles framed and reflected. (The same wall construction appears on the other side of this block, on the north wall of the atrium, but not tilted from the vertical.)

The basic materials of the curtain walls follow the overall design policy of using straightforward, industrially produced materials, rather than any that could be construed as luxurious or monumental. The curtain walls are given a consistency, within their varied configurations, by the use of aluminum painted a shade of white and a uniform type of precast concrete. The white-painted metal, played against the gray of the glazing, produces an overall silvery image and reduces the apparent weight of the complex. The concrete establishes a visual link with the walls of the two existing buildings—one limestone, the other travertine.

The precast concrete of the curtain walls appears in the form of vertical piers. Fabricated in two-story-high sections, these piers were cast in forms made of soft pine boards, with the edges of the boards chamfered to generate a series of vertical ridges on their faces that lend them texture and shadow pattern. This carefully made formwork was made economically feasible by laminating the boards and fastening them to plywood form liners to make possible repeated re-use. After mock-ups had been produced to the satisfaction of the design team, using headless finishing nails, the precaster inadvertently used nails with heads to fasten the boards to the first batch of forms. Because the wood expands during concrete hydration, the nail heads produced visible dimples in the finished piers; the design team accepted 43 of these for use on the upper floors of phase one construction, where only the most determined construction critics could spot them.

The curtain wall glazing is 20 percent reflective, a degree of reflection carefully adjusted to mask the distinction between spandrels and windows, while still looking transparent. Behind the subtle adjustment of the glass type lies the firm's substantial experience at fine-tuning the apparent reflectivity of glass. This building closely follows the type of glazing developed for the Goldman Sachs building in London. In the sandwich of the insulating glass lights, the reflective coating is on the outer surface of the inner layer of glass; all the glass is of a low-reflectance type. The result is a surface that looks neither ominously dark nor too metallic—or "tinny."

For this building, the glass manufacturers, working closely with KPF, produced a customized three-coat application for the number-three surface of the insulated glazing units. This consisted of a layer of tin oxide, a layer of stainless steel, and a layer of titanium dioxide. Over 30 samples were produced before a composition was formulated to achieve the design team's objective. The resulting product was cost effective, since no spandrel glass was needed where the curtain wall passes slab edges and other opaque components.

KPF worked directly with curtain wall manufacturers, from the early design phases, to develop standardized aluminum extrusions that are shared among seven distinct types of curtain wall.

These curtain walls also include operable windows, which have rarely appeared in recent United States urban office buildings. The architects were in the design development phase of work when members of the bank's staff — including particularly Europeans—persuaded the bank management to require operable windows. The windows were incorporated without visibly changing the design, but at additional cost. For the distinctive wall of the H Street front, operable vents within the horizontal wall members were used instead of operable windows.

For the top floor Executive Conference Room overlooking Pennsylvania Avenue, the architects developed an insulating glass unit $2\frac{1}{2}$ inches thick, with blinds hermetically sealed between its two layers of glazing. They are motorized for optimal light control in a space where dramatic views are an asset, but summer brings the problem of low late afternoon sunlight and glare to the north-facing glass.

1 North elevation
2 West elevation

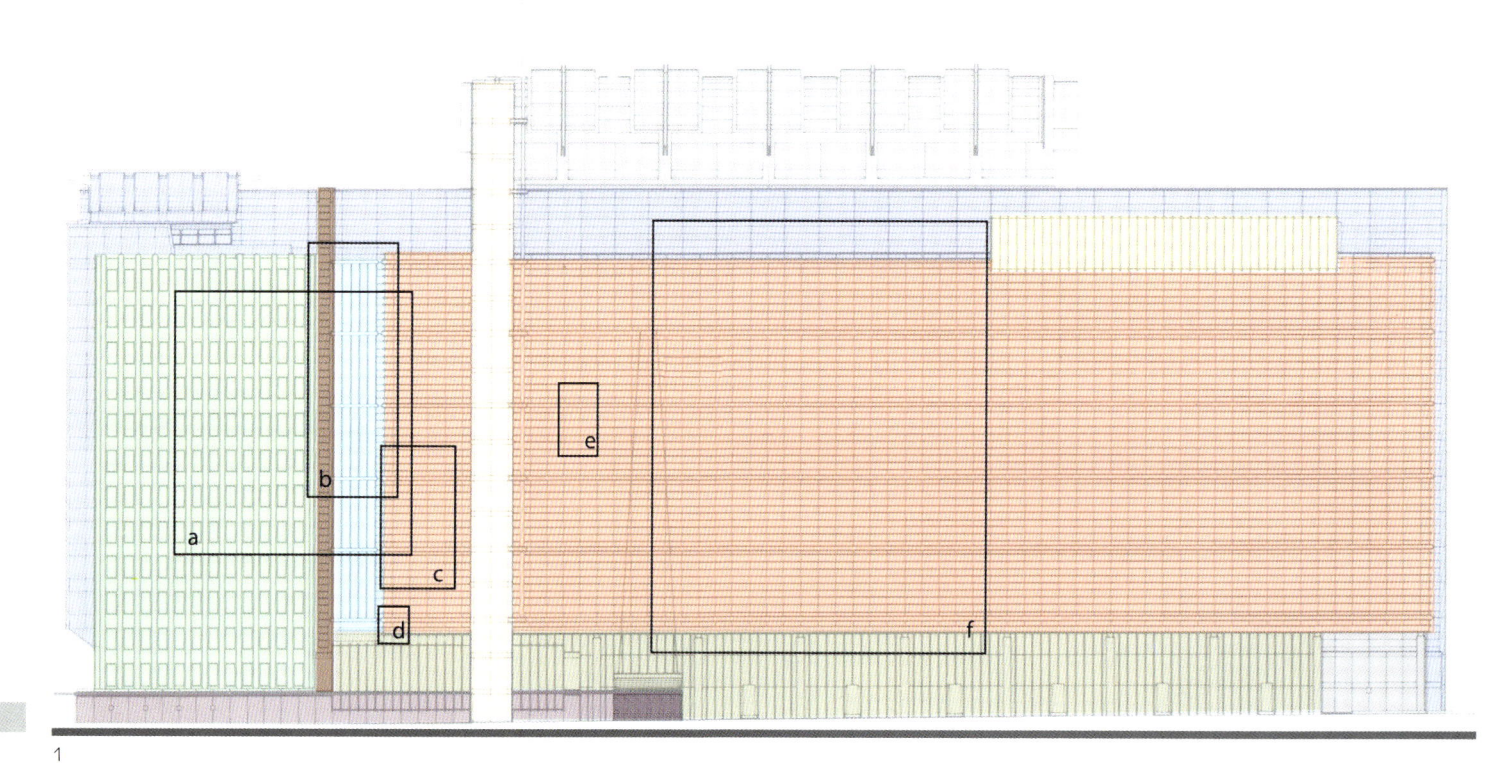

- Travertine facade of existing building by SOM
- Board-formed concrete, painted aluminum and glass
- Board-formed concrete, painted aluminum and glass with projecting snap caps
- Painted aluminum and glass with expressed vertical fins
- Existing Indiana limestone
- Painted aluminum outriggers
- Zipper wall: Painted aluminum and glass
- Painted aluminum panels and glass
- Painted aluminum panels
- Painted aluminum and glass clerestory
- Painted aluminum
- Painted metal and glass
- Precast board-formed concrete
- Restoration of existing limestone façade
- Storefront: Painted aluminum and glass with projecting fins on a precast board-formed concrete wainscot with painted aluminum canopy above
- Lobby storefront: Painted aluminum and glass
- Entries: Clear natural anodized vertically ribbed aluminum panels with frames for display

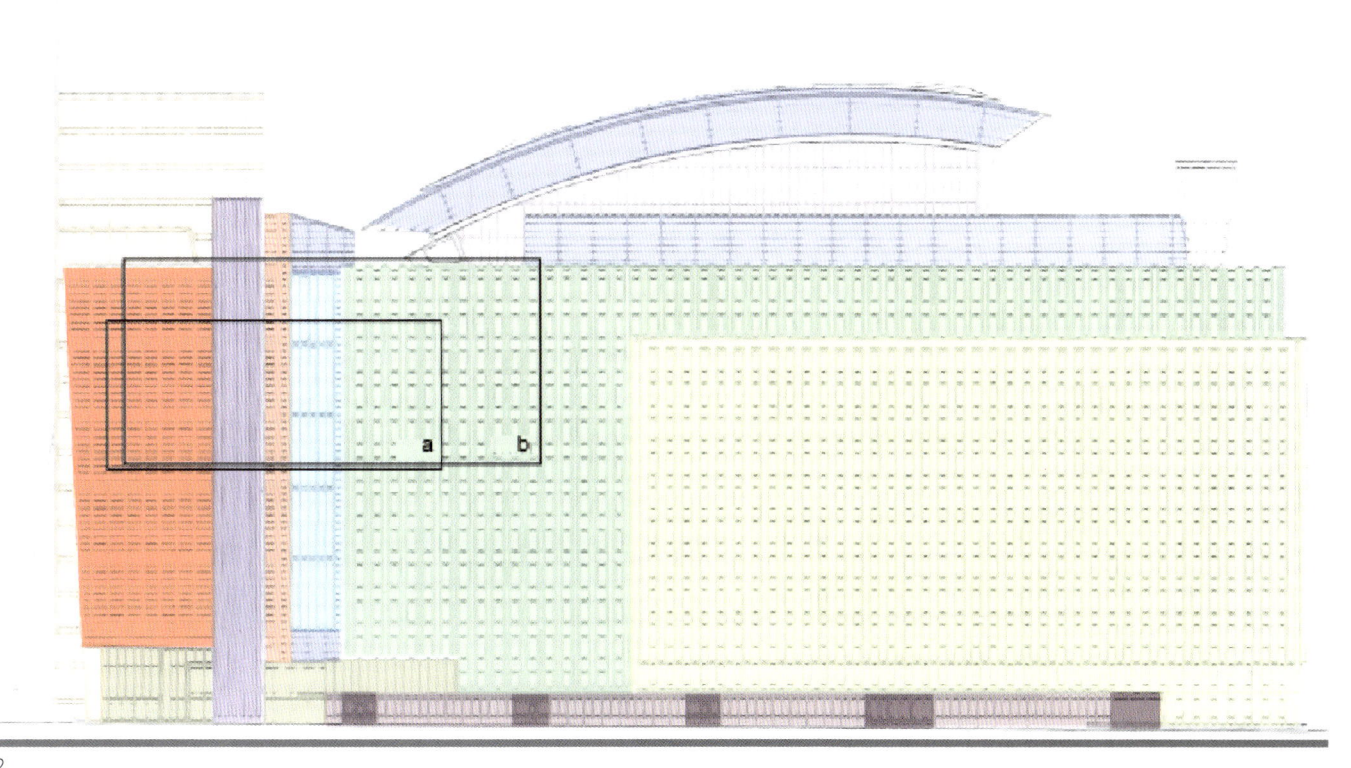

3 South elevation
4 East elevation

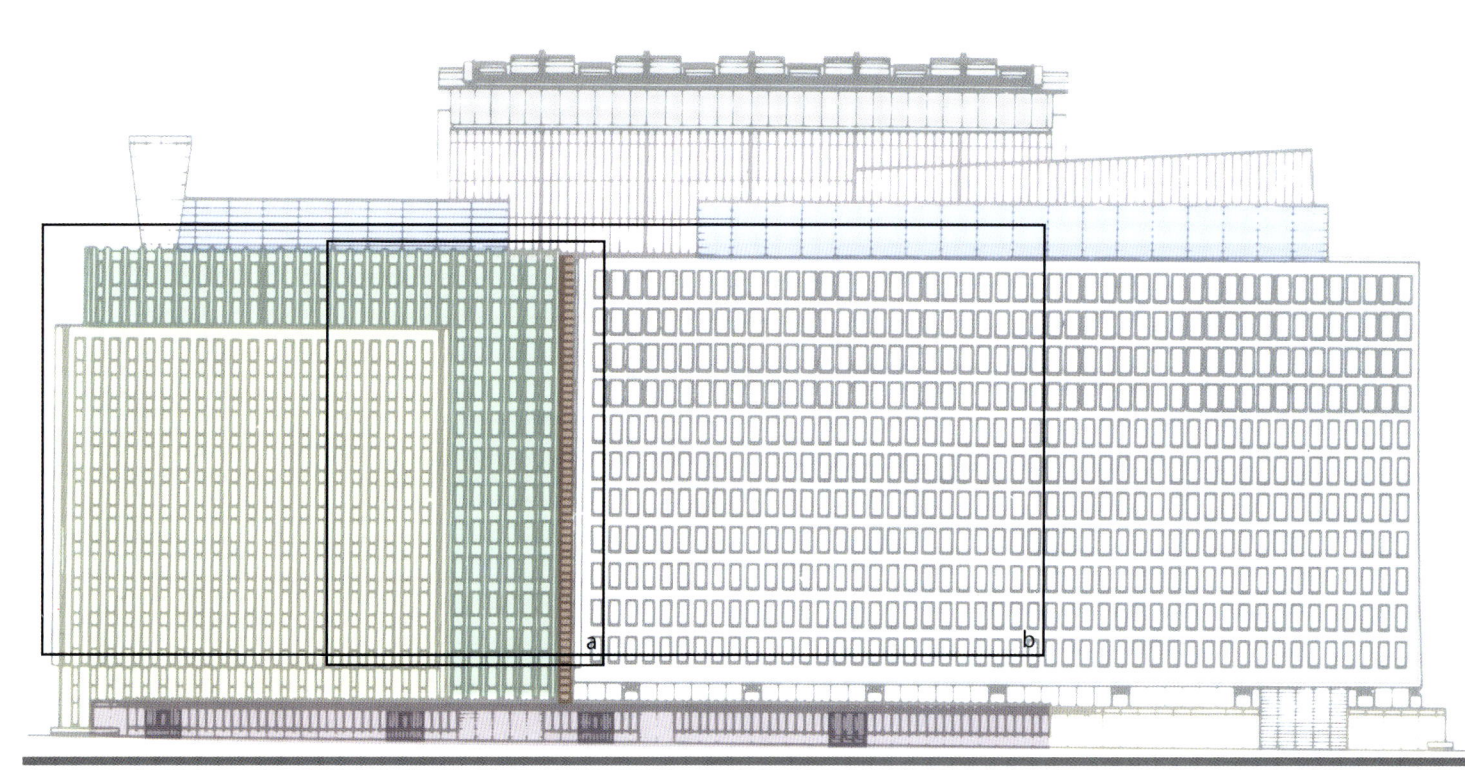

4

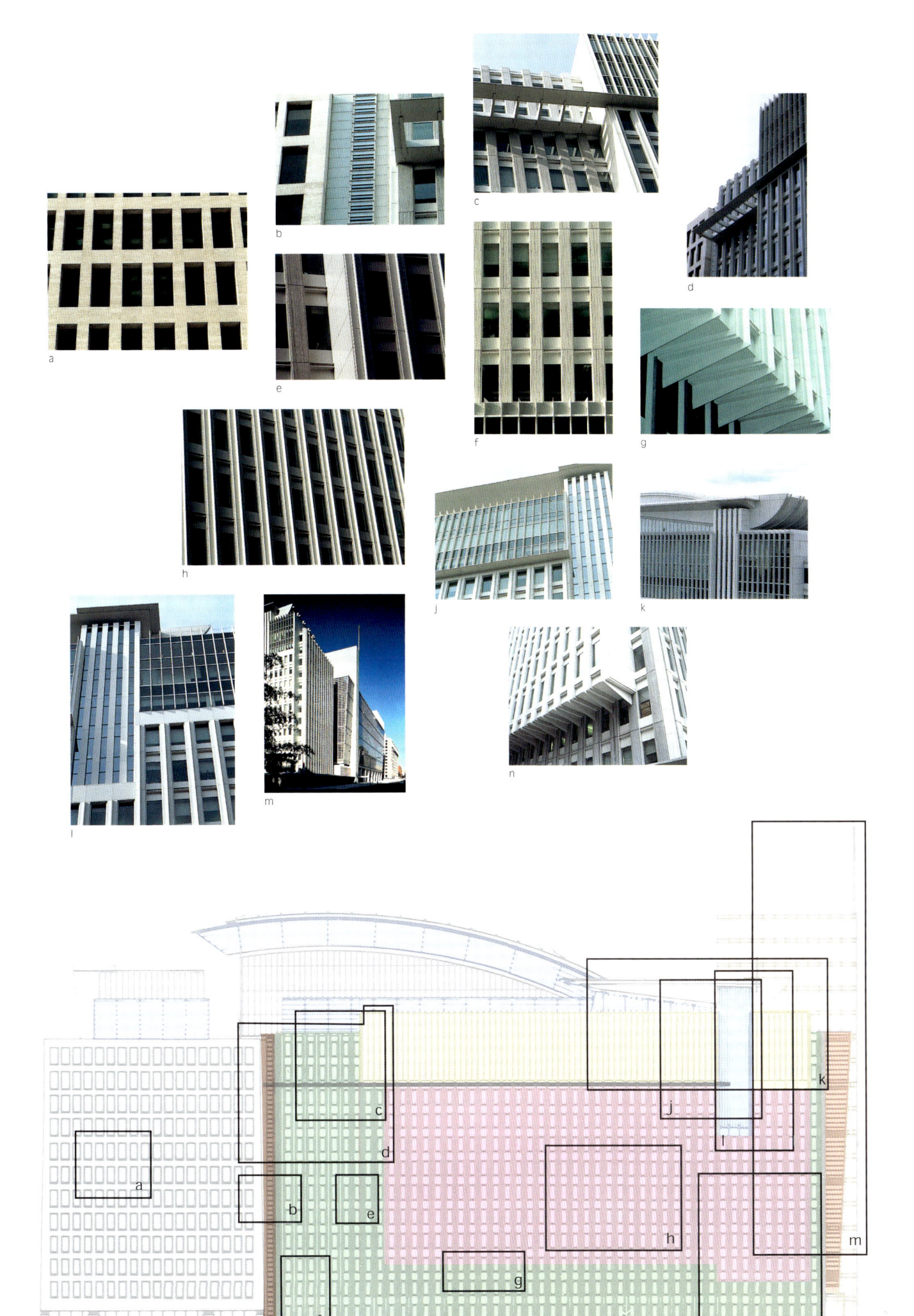

5

6   7

5   Glass and aluminum curtain wall with painted aluminum horizontal outriggers at left; vertical strip with aluminum fins; precast vertical piers with aluminum spandrels at right. (West elevation, photo b)

6   Recess separating glass and painted aluminum office curtain wall, above, from glass and painted aluminum lobby wall, below. (North elevation, photo d)

7   Glass and aluminum curtain wall with horizontal outriggers on H Street front. (North elevation, photo c)

8   New precast concrete, aluminum, and glass curtain wall between 1967 limestone wall of E Building, at left, and 1968 travertine wall of D Building, at right. (South elevation, photo a)

9   Conjunction of D Building wall, at left, concrete and aluminum Phase 1 office walls, at center and lower right, and wall with deep aluminum fins, at upper right. (East elevation, photo d)

10 Travertine-clad wall of 1968 D Building, at left; new zipper wall of painted aluminum and glass, at center; office curtain wall with precast piers, at right. (East elevation, photo b)

SPECIFIC SPACES

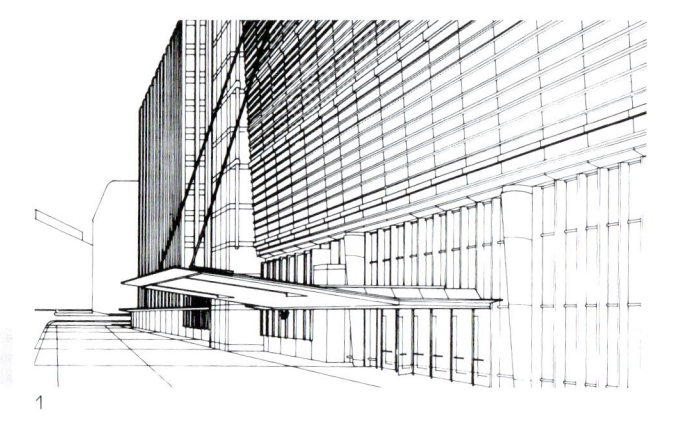

Entrance and Lobby

Although the World Bank has entrances for the convenience of staff on all four abutting streets, the H Street entry is the principal one, used by visitors to the bank. This main entrance and the lobby just inside are carefully calibrated to indicate that the bank is a special institution, without any hint of aggrandizement. This entry point is announced from a distance by an ample but discreet canopy, suspended by long cables anchored to the façade 10 stories above the street. While the cable support is a striking device, it is executed in an understated way, making the cables and connections no more visible than necessary. This combination of the unexpected and the restrained presents, in effect, a succinct preview of the entire complex.

Inside the main entrance, one finds a lobby that is also ample yet understated. The eye is first led to the pool of daylight in the atrium, straight ahead. While the bank must require all visitors to be identified and pass through security gates, the actual gates present a minimal visual intrusion as the visitor moves ahead. The security desk, where visitors check in and receive badges, stands discreetly to one side of the entry route, the whole arrangement stressing the acts of welcoming and assistance, rather than exclusion.

1 Drawing of main H Street entrance with cable-suspended canopy.
2 Main entrance showing effect of skylights in canopy.
3 Entire set of main entrance doors.
4 Detail of main entrance doors.

5 Portion of aluminum-leaf-clad ceiling in main lobby.
6 Main lobby looking toward reception desk.
7 Elevator doors showing designs in stainless steel.
8 Passage to main elevators with stairs to upper and lower level.
9 Stepped passage connecting lobby and 18th Street entrance.

8

9

Although the lobby is the equivalent of three office floors in height, it reads visually as a low transition between the exterior and the 150-foot-high atrium ahead. This sequence of spatial compression and release is sensitively enhanced by the lobby ceiling's gentle convex curve. Clad in aluminum leaf this ceiling illuminates the lobby softly with diffused reflections of daylight both from outside and from the atrium.

Atrium

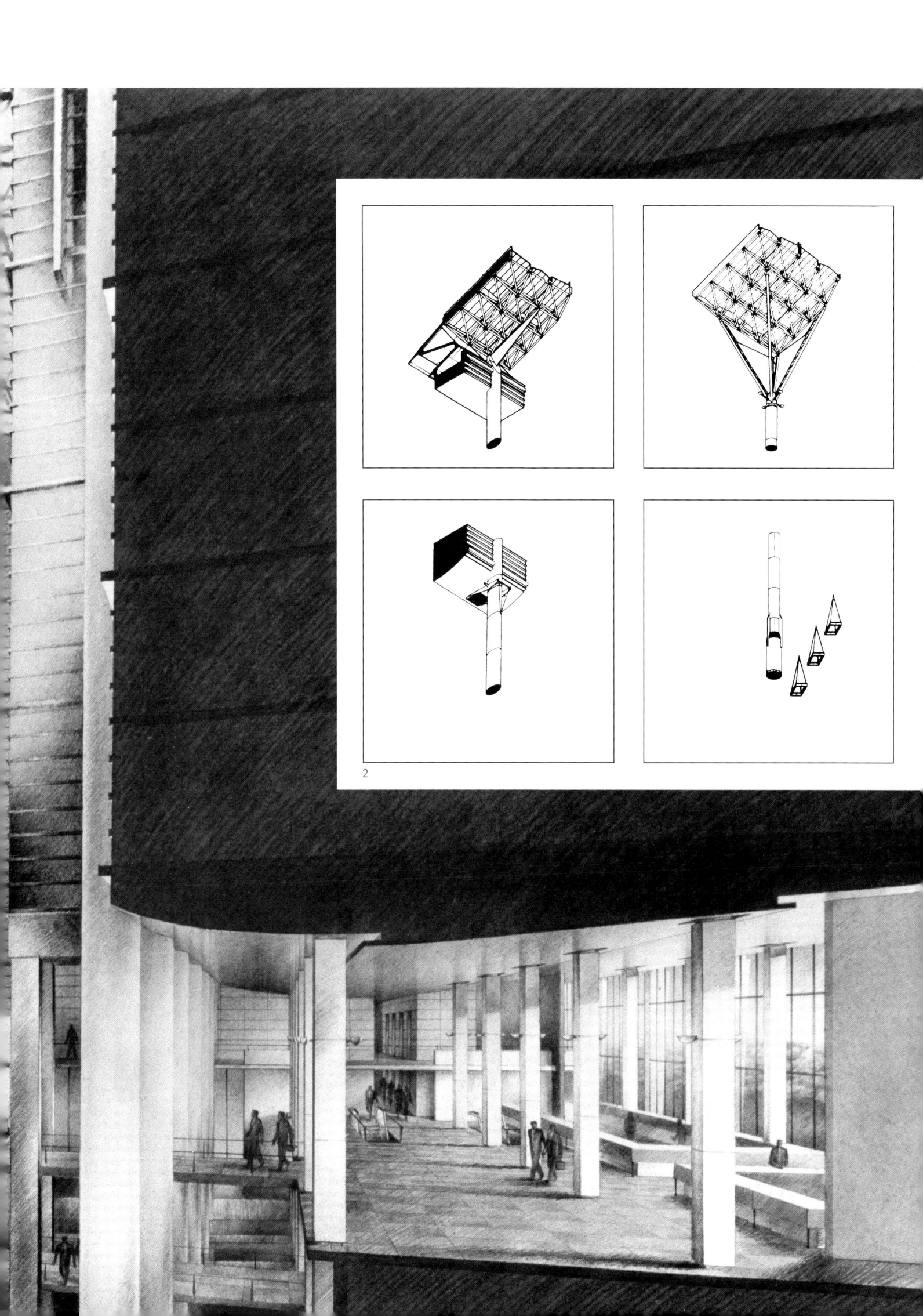

2

The bank's central atrium is a light-filled space, the interior equivalent of a town square for the thousands of people who work in the building and visit it daily. Measuring 150 feet square and 150 feet high, the atrium is made all the more exhilarating to those entering the building by the sequence that leads to it: a very low entrance canopy, a somewhat higher lobby with a concave, aluminum-coated ceiling that visibly compresses the space one passes through then releases it as the full height and expanse of the atrium become visible.

Changes in the atrium's floor level, both up and down from street level, along with stairs and various vertical elements—including a stack of conference rooms forming a campanile—reinforce the feeling of an actual urban space, rather than an interior. These elements mediate the atrium's scale and also succeed in populating it, so that it does not seem empty, even to a lone visitor. Yet the various bridges, terraces, and alcoves also enhance its use for large gatherings.

Carved out of the atrium floor is a light well extending down two stories to light the dining areas, the travel office, and the credit union. Though the area of this light well is not large in relation to the atrium, distinctive features make it a very prominent element in the experience of the building. At one point water from a linear reflecting pool along one side of the atrium spills 28 feet down into the pool that lines the bottom of the well; a nearby bridge to the employee dining area offers an appealing view of the waterfall and an opportunity to enjoy its sound at close range.

The curtain walls of the various building volumes facing the atrium have been carefully adjusted to provide some visual variety without distraction. The atrium sides of the two older buildings have both been altered; the E Building was widened an entire bay and the slightly battered wall of the D Building was extended to become a true vertical. The predominantly vertical pattern of all these walls masks the differences in floor levels behind them. The colors of the surfaces, white and pale neutrals, along with the restrained, mostly repetitive surfaces, all have the visual qualities of not just any urban scene, but a Washington streetscape in particular.

The roof is supported on the new construction, but at the far end, where existing structures could not carry the additional load, it is impressively supported on five tall cylindrical concrete columns, branching expressively into steel struts where they support the roof. The cost of the roof and the structure supporting it are offset in part by reduced costs for heating and air conditioning of the surrounding spaces.

Conceived as a gathering place, the atrium has gradually accommodated a growing agenda of events. Cultural activities, exhibits, a "development marketplace" and numerous community outreach events now continually animate the atrium.

Previous pages:
1   Perspective from final competition design, showing atrium at left, main lobby at right.
2   Key elements of atrium: at left, structural column meeting lobby soffit (lower drawing) and space frame roof (upper drawing); at right, freestanding concrete column, with translucent pyramids (lower drawing) and supporting space frame roof (upper drawing).

Opposite:
At center of World Bank, skylighted atrium 150 feet square and 150 feet high to peak of space-frame roof.

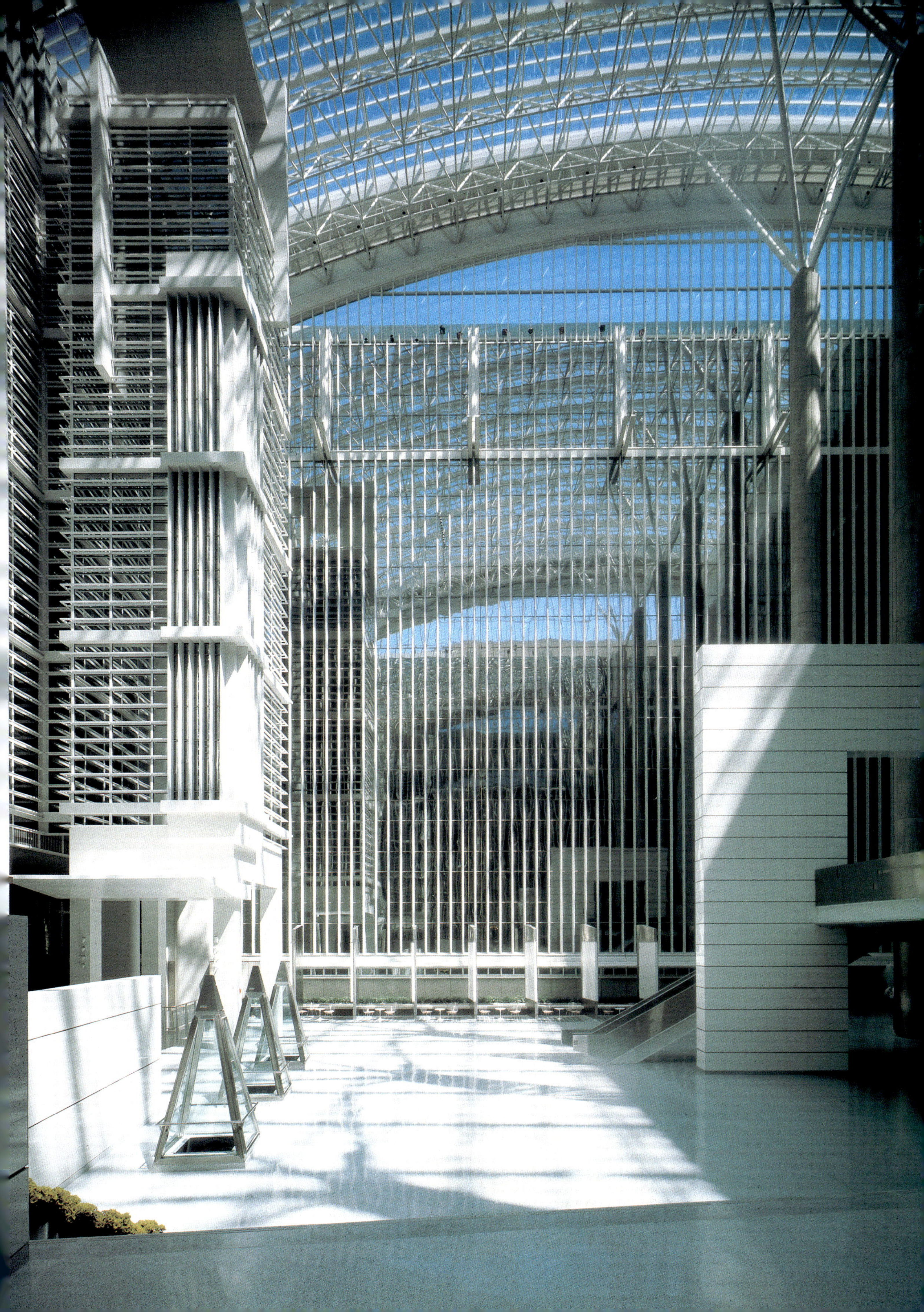

4

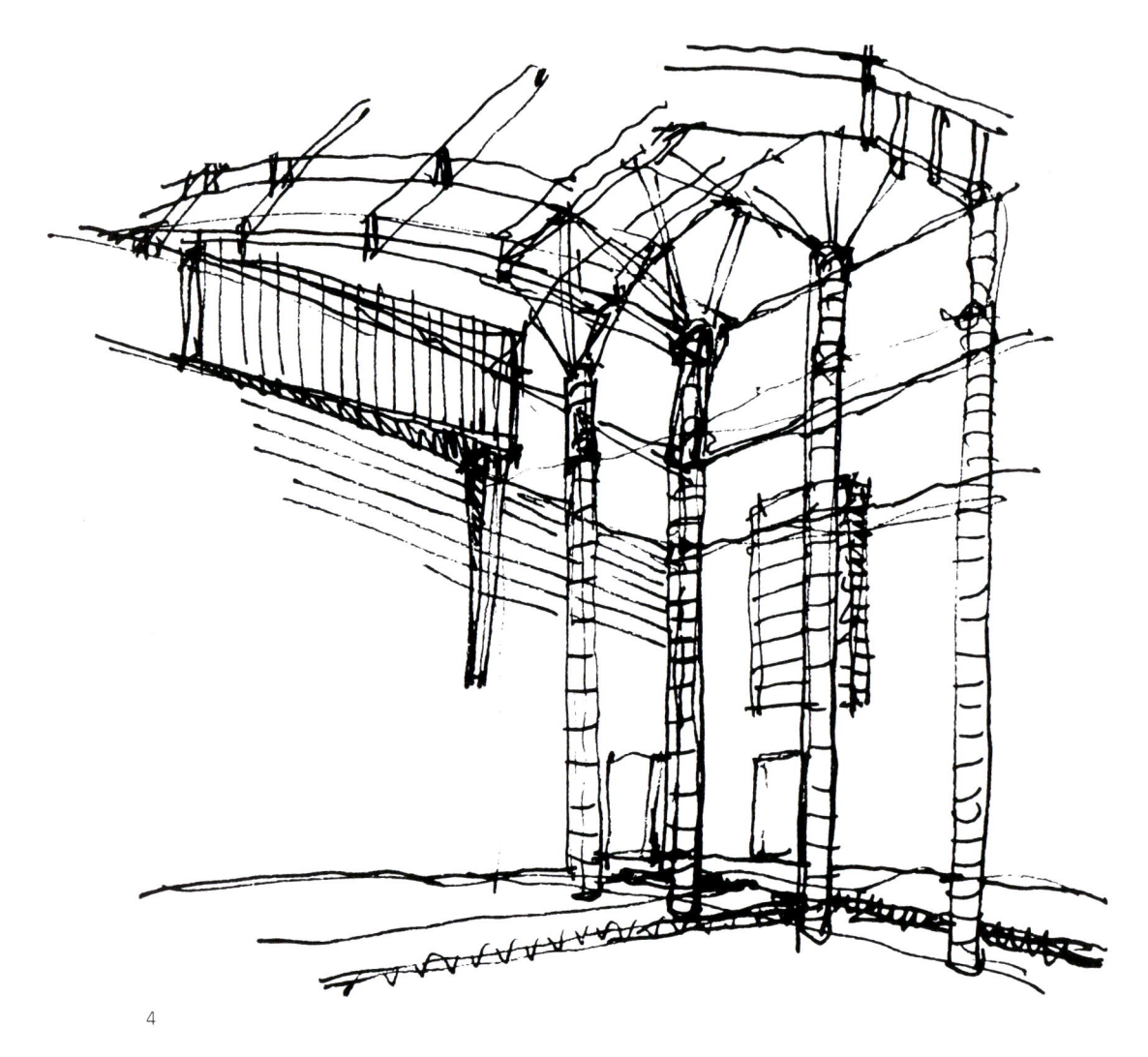

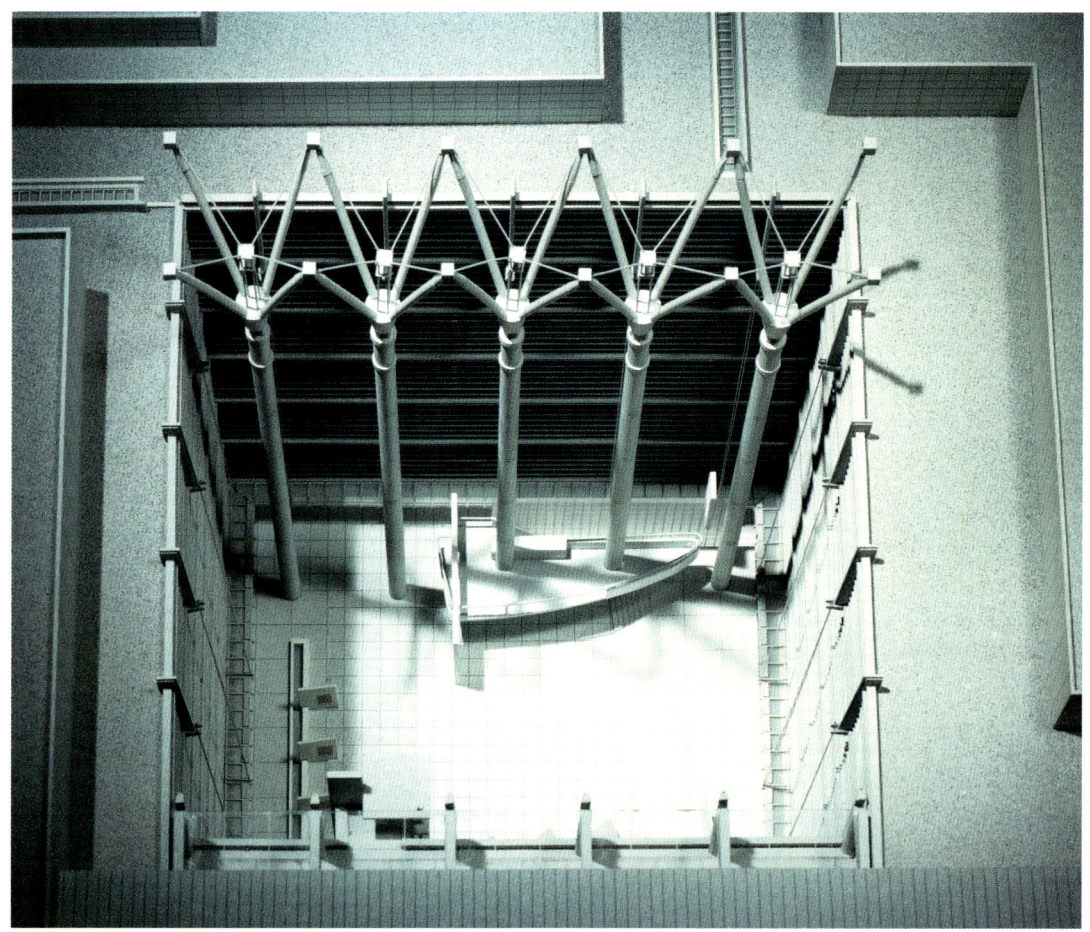

5

4   Early sketch of atrium, with branching columns.
5   Final competition model of atrium, showing five columns and central raised terrace.
6   Perspective of branching columns from final competition drawings.
7   Early sketch of atrium, showing columns supporting curved space-frame roof.

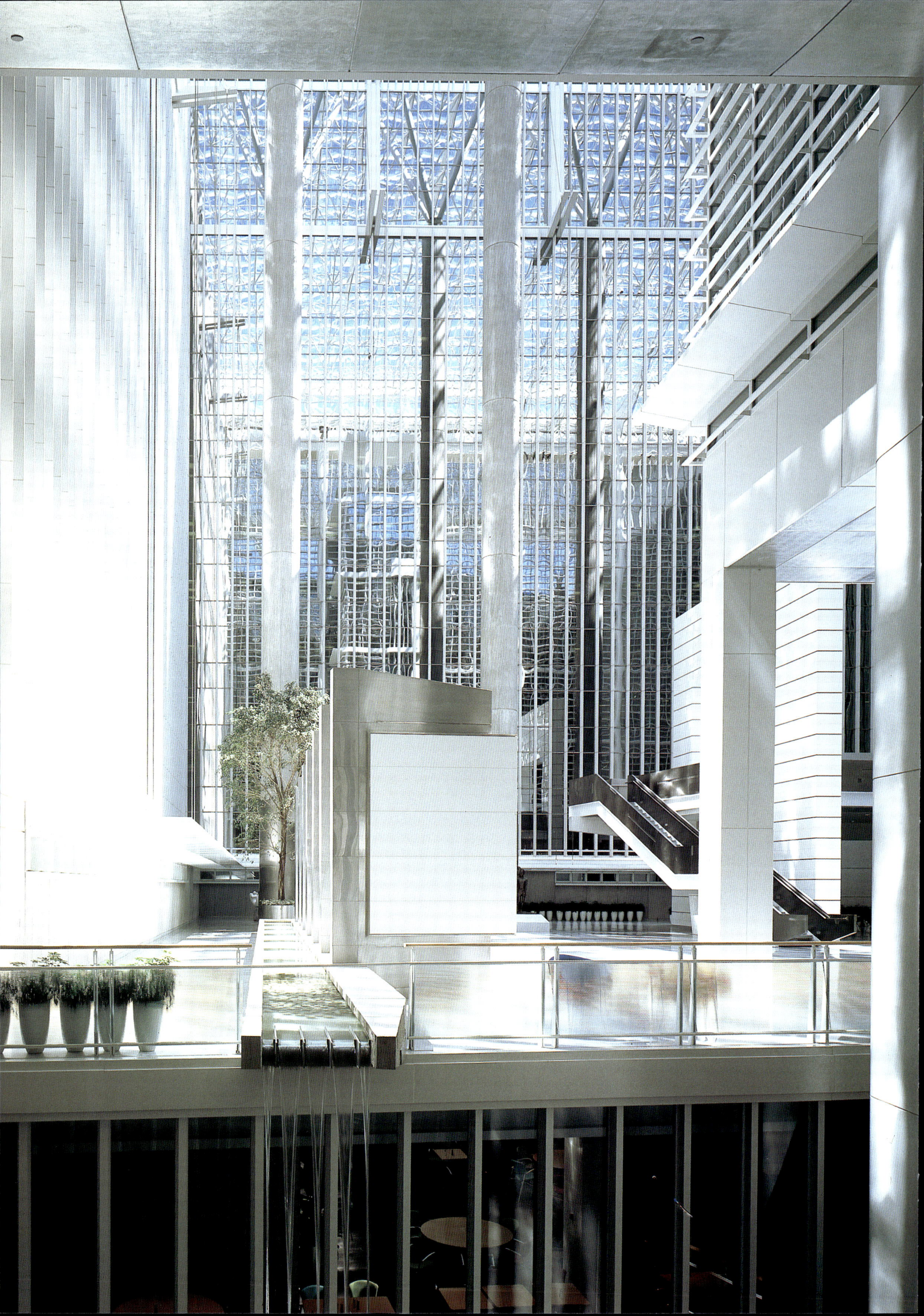

Opposite:
Water trough along one side of atrium spilling into light well

9   Atrium's impressive size broken down to human scale by terraces, stairs, and series of panels (foreground) that can accommodate temporary displays.

10 Panels along one side of atrium defining seating alcoves, adaptable for informational displays at events related to international commerce.

Opposite:
Stack of conference rooms forming tower in one corner of atrium.

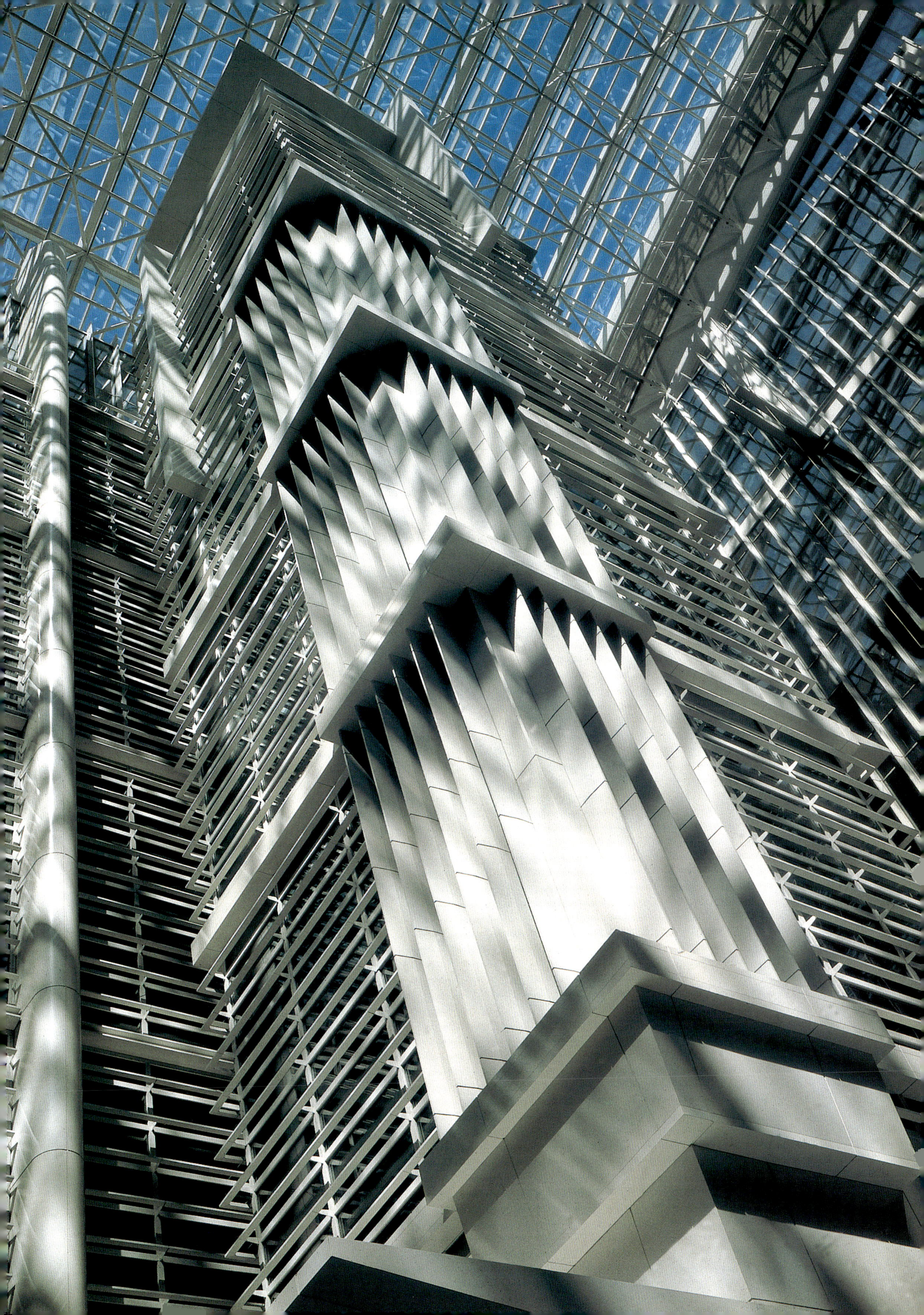

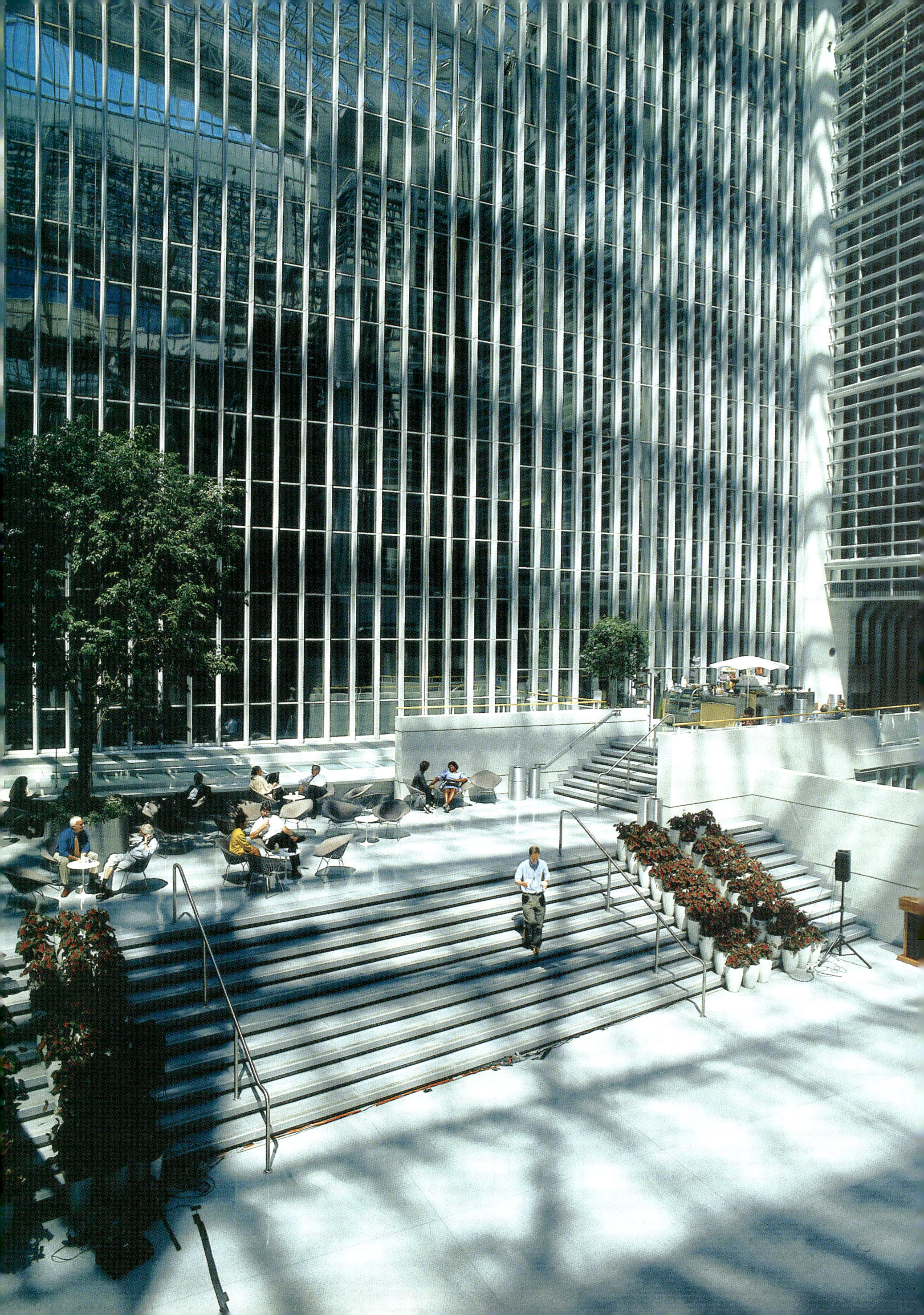

Opposite:
Terraces along side of
atrium, with coffee bar
on upper level.
13 Coffee bar terrace in corner, accessible from main elevators.
14 Working break on atrium terrace.
15 Informal staff gathering on terrace.

89

16 At one corner of atrium, passage to E Building elevators and 19th Street.
17 Quiet area at edge of atrium, along linear pool.
18 Glazed pyramids on atrium floor that supply daylight to cafeteria below and glow in evening with artificial light.

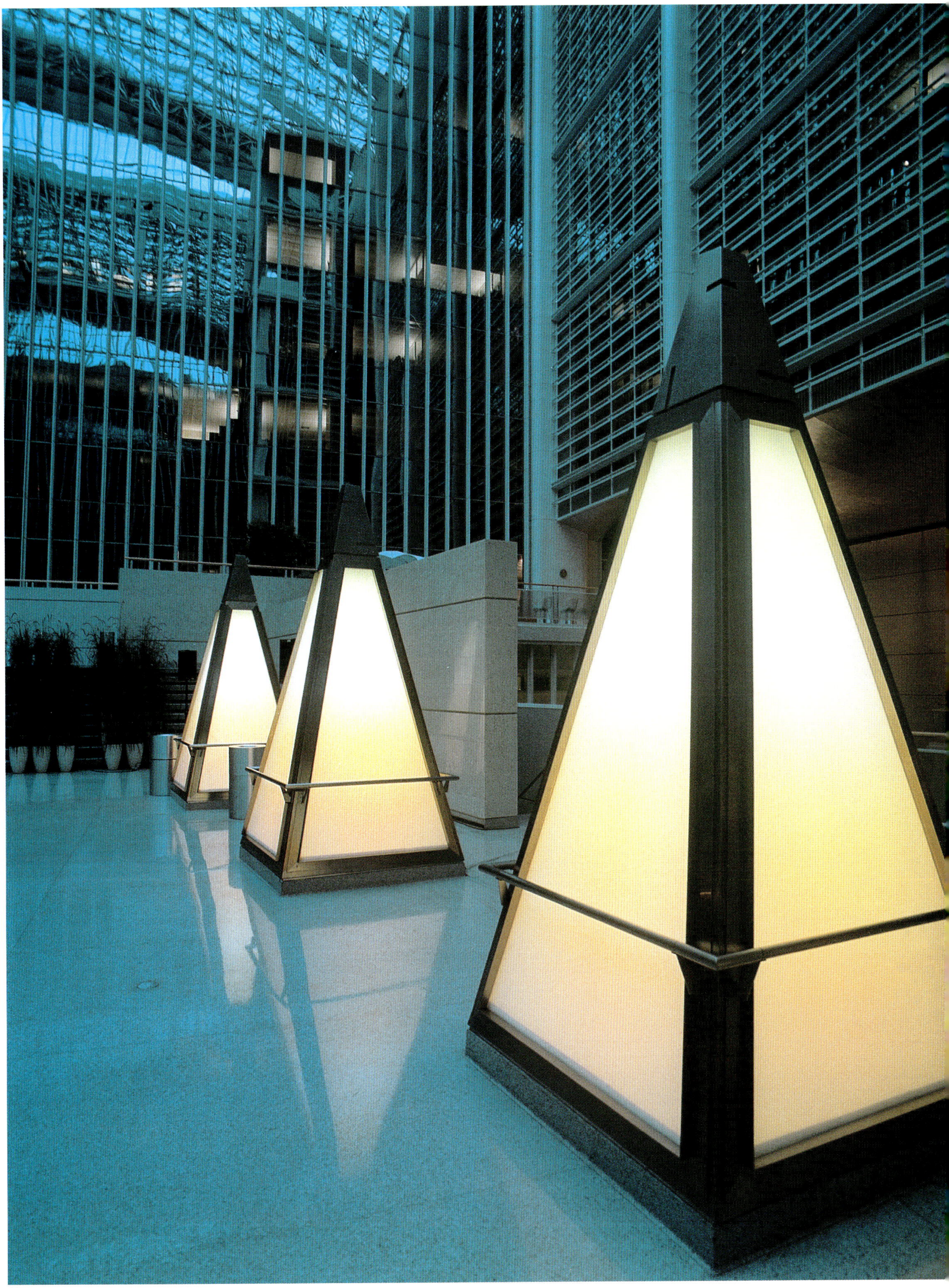

19

19 Light well extending below atrium floor level, with glazed cafeteria wall at center, cafeteria terrace at right.
20 View from footbridge crossing light well to cafeteria.

Following pages:
21 Linear atrium pool supplying waterfall that plunges into light well.
22 Waterfall dropping two stories, past cafeteria windows, into pool at bottom of light well.

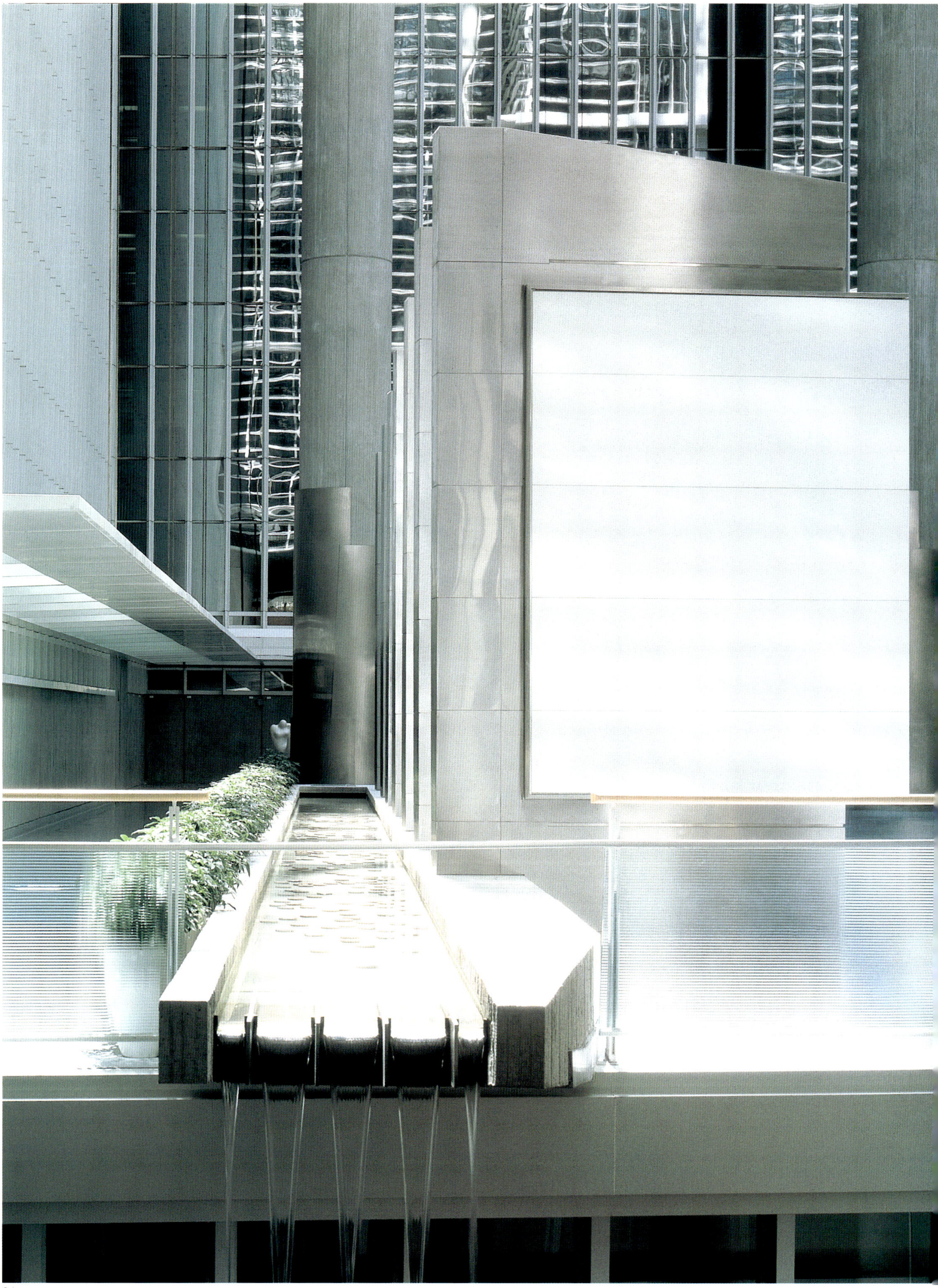

21

22

23 Overlooking light well and pool: coffee bar terrace at top and cafeteria terrace below.
24 Sunlighted pool at base of light well, with cafeteria terrace.

Opposite:
View up from cafeteria terrace extending to skylighted atrium roof.

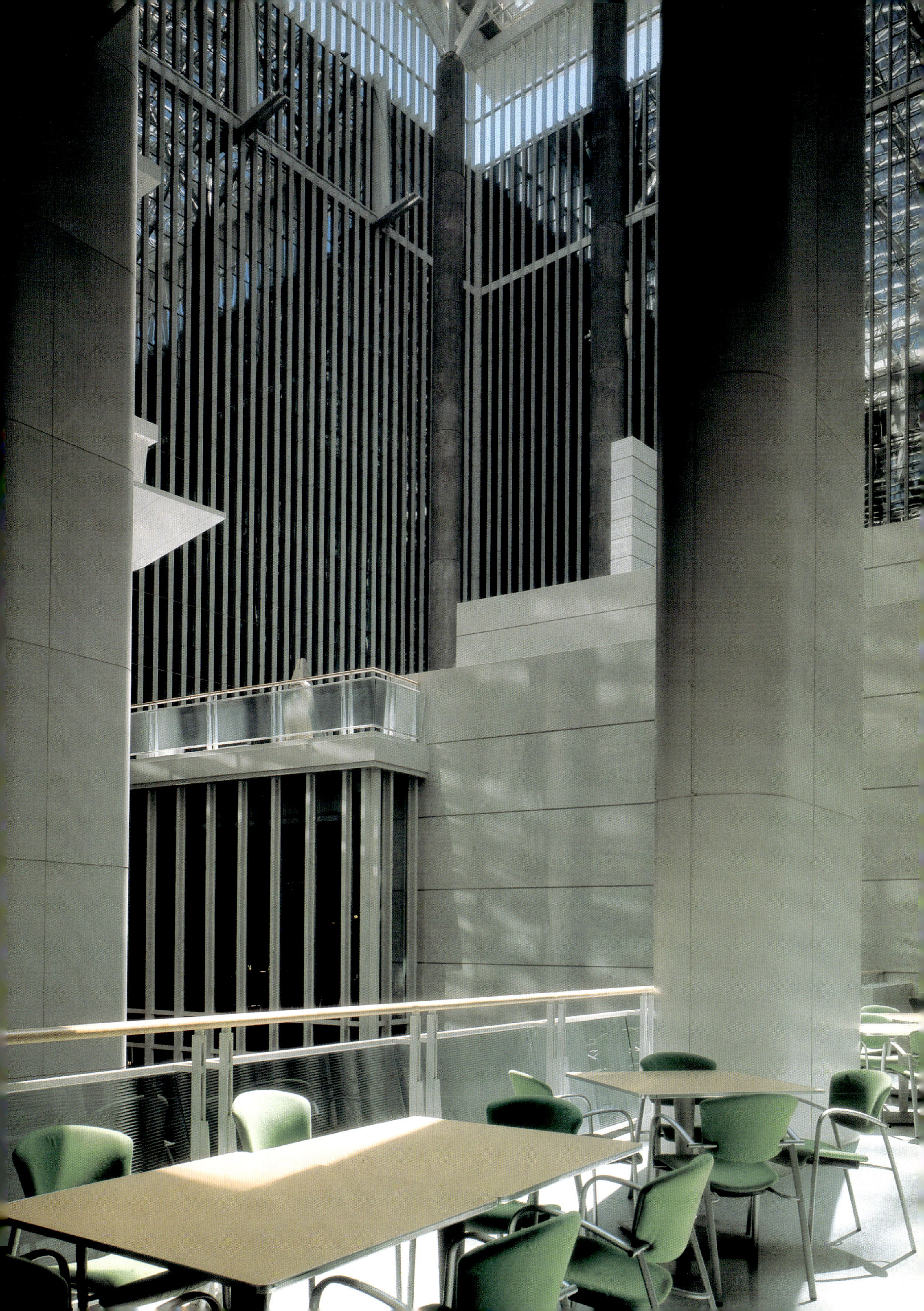

Typical Offices

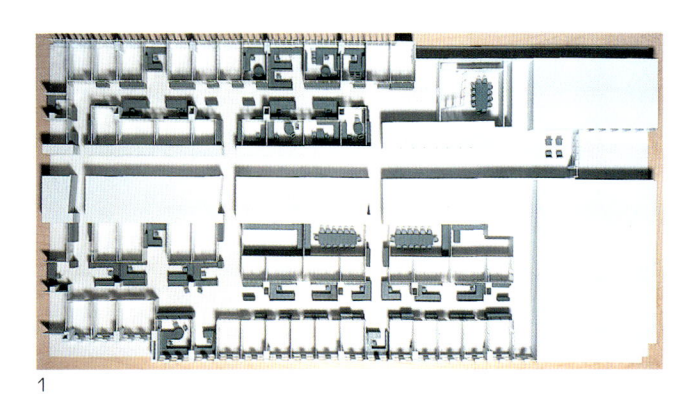

1

As soon as the KPF design was accepted, members of the bank's staff began working closely with the architects to ensure that the offices would suit their particular requirements. A number of bank staff members spent one or two days a week at KPF's New York offices for roughly a year during the design development phase.

The bank's building team and the architects agreed from the outset of their collaboration that the office floors should have dedicated corridors, rather than simply paths threading through flexible office space. For this organization, it was thought preferable to have central corridors with walls, which provide essential locations for the numerous vertical ducts and volume control boxes required for this building's air-conditioning system. Such corridors take up floor space and reduce the flexibility of layout, but they minimize distraction from people simply passing through and reinforce department identity. Their walls can be interrupted for clear-cut entries to each department and their surfaces used for the display of pertinent art and documents.

To serve their international workforce, the offices had to adhere to a hierarchy of standard types keyed to employment grades. They also had to allow for an exceptional degree of relocation, as departments grow, shrink, and reorganize, and as staff members rotate between headquarters and field assignments. (Any year, 3,000 to 4,000 of the bank's worldwide staff of about 10,000 are relocated.) A high degree of standardization among the offices makes possible a lot of shifting of personnel without physically reconfiguring the offices. But offices can be reconfigured readily because all are made up of a small number of standardized elements.

The office design had to account for the 8-foot 1-inch ceiling heights—low for an organization of this type, but common in Washington because of its rigid building height limits. Because of the expectations of the bank's international staff, there was a greater concern than in many Washington buildings for daylight to penetrate the workspaces beyond the exterior private offices. One crucial design decision was to have glazed clerestories for all office partitions, with some glass panels below as well, so that natural light would be dispersed throughout the floor and there would be a feeling of openness.

During the design process, full-scale mock-ups were built, and bank employees worked in them for several months, providing accurate feedback. Consultation with representative employees and feedback from the mock-ups resulted in important adjustment to glass areas in the partitions and to indirect lighting details.

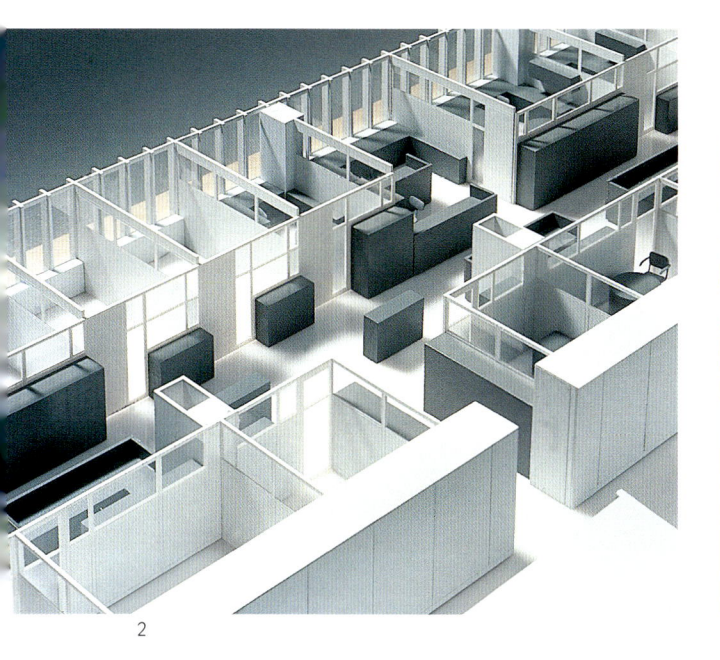

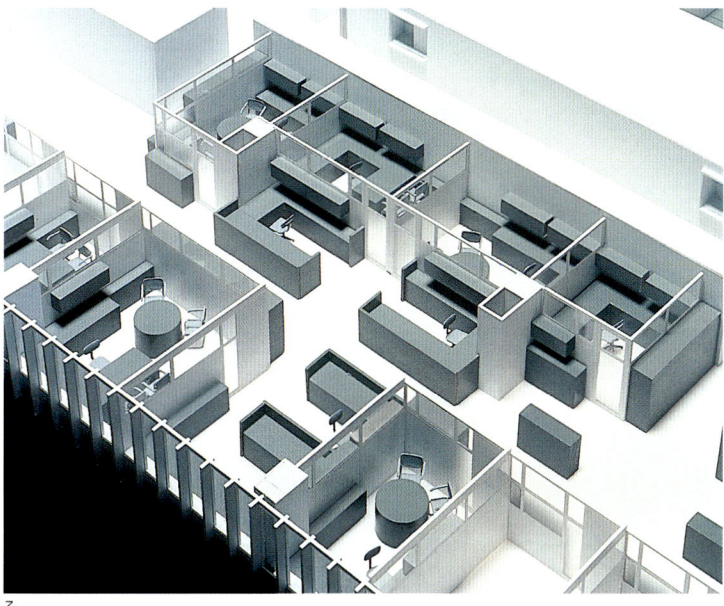

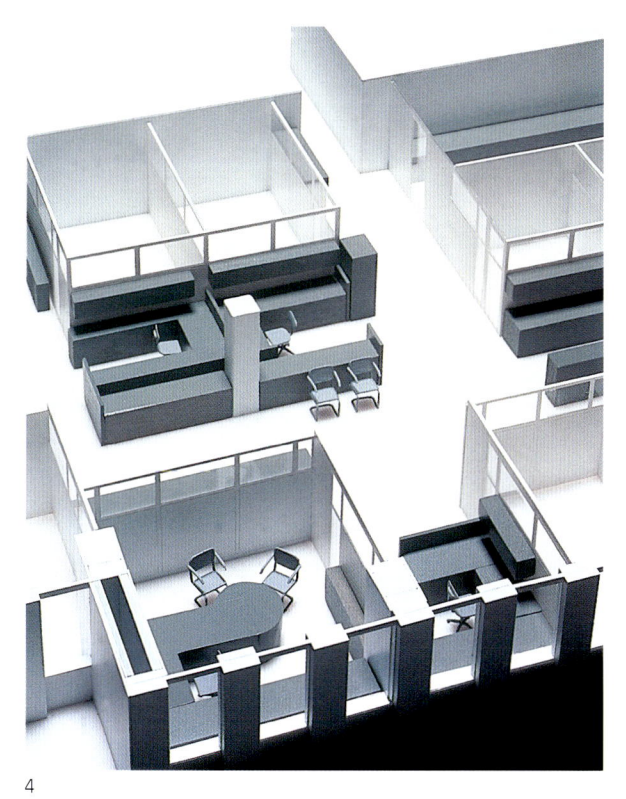

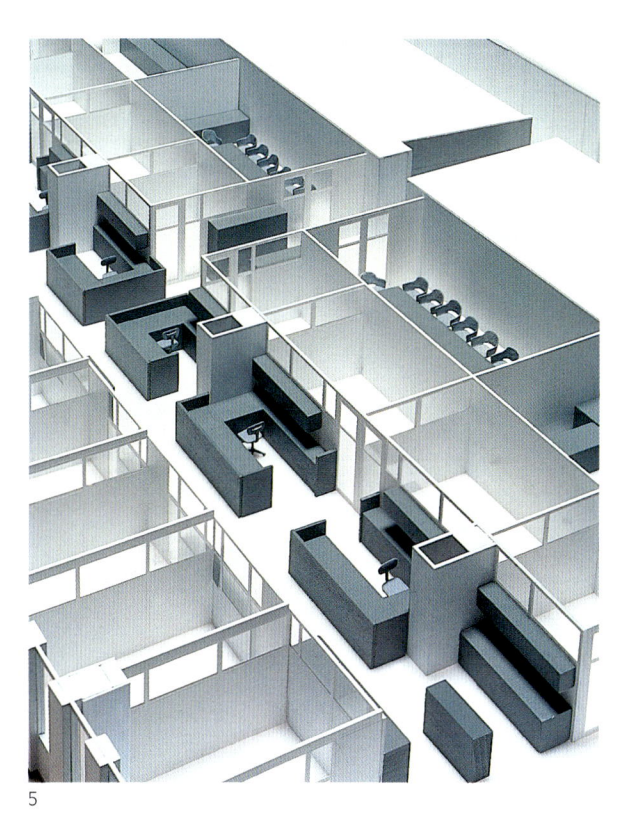

1. Model showing variety of layouts on typical office floor.
2. Final competition model, portion of typical office floor.
3. Model showing alternative office layout, windows in foreground.
4. Detail, model of one possible office layout.
5. Model of office layout with high ratio of private offices.

99

6 Plan showing portion of representative department, with elevators, lobby, and other shared spaces.
7 Plan of typical office "neighborhood."
8 Plan of office "neighborhood," showing possible specialized layout.
9 Office "neighborhood" with high ratio of open office workstations.

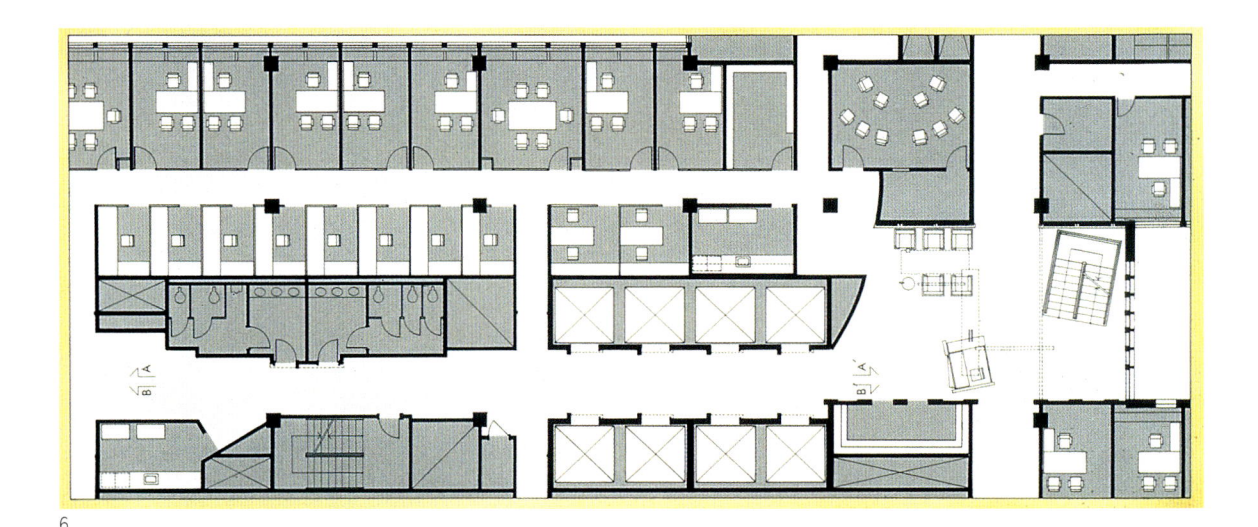

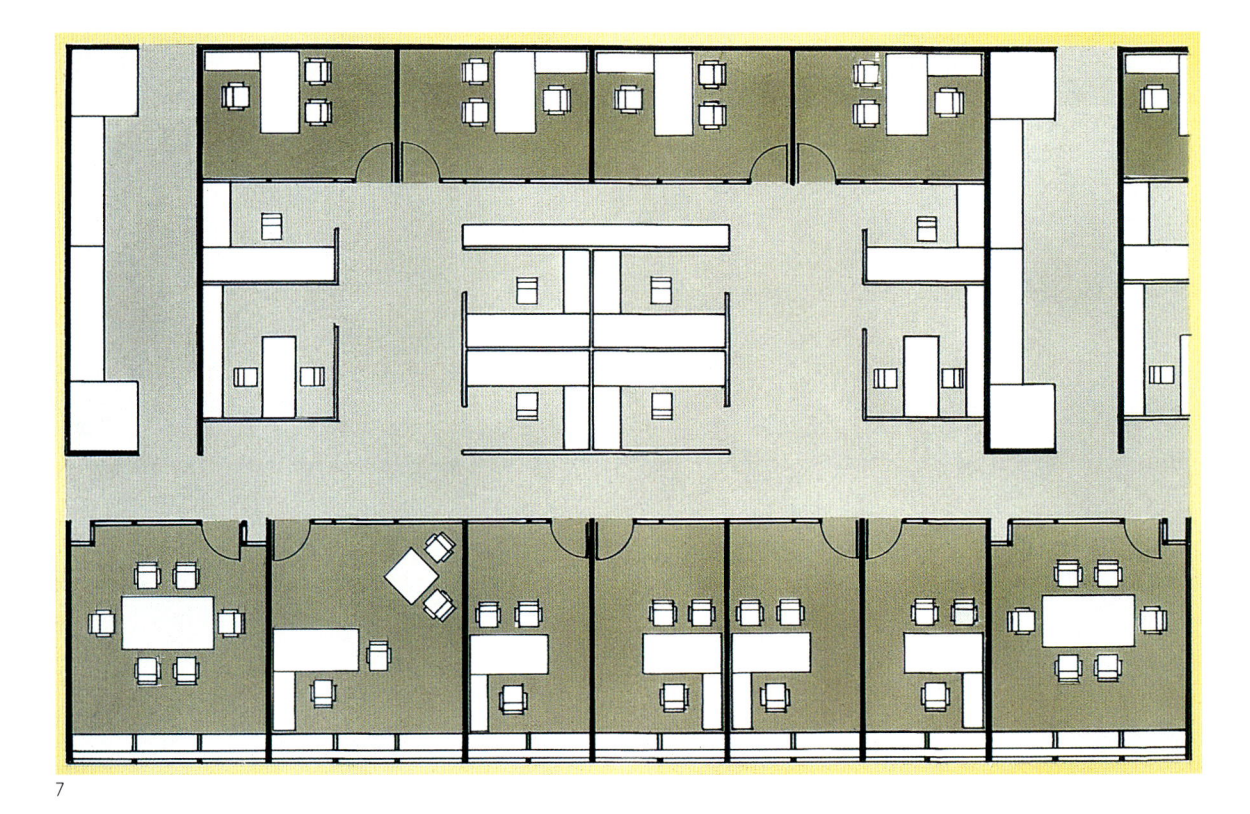

6

7

8

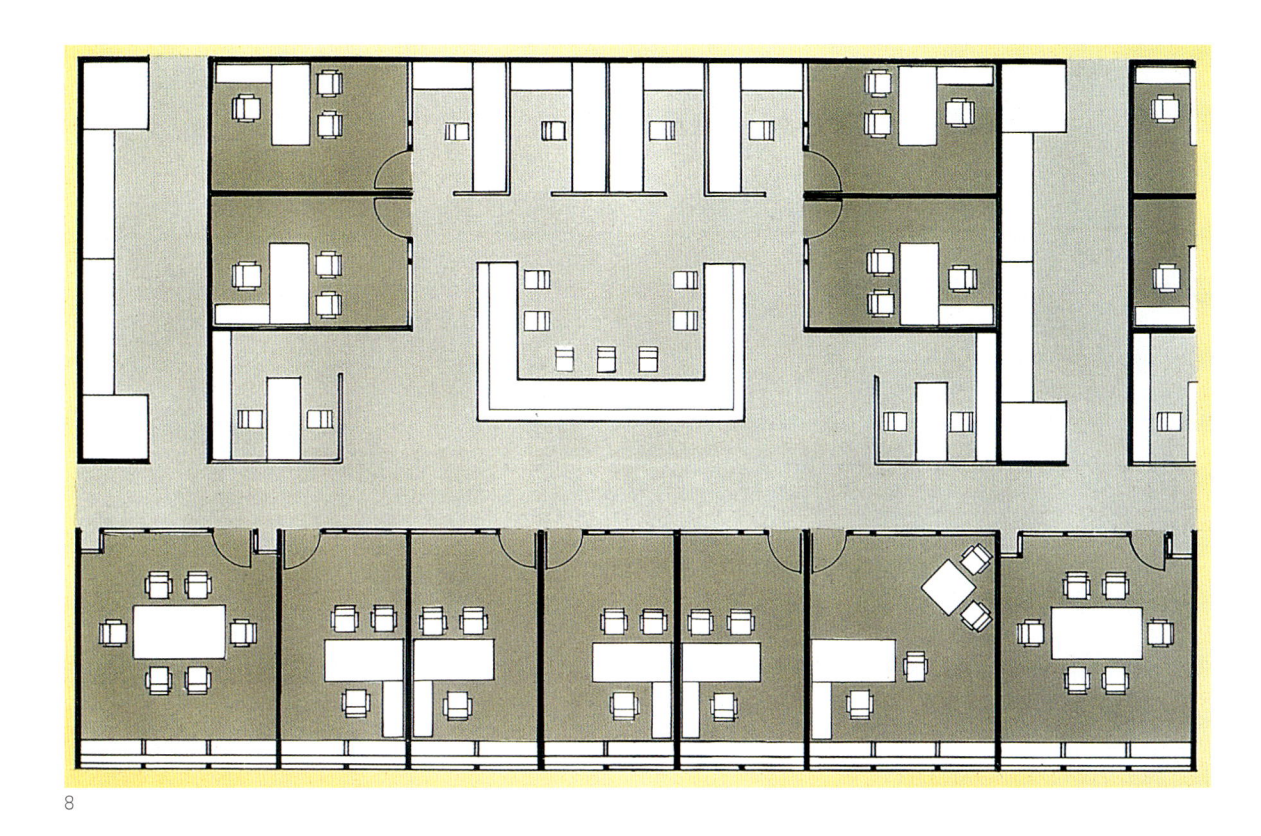

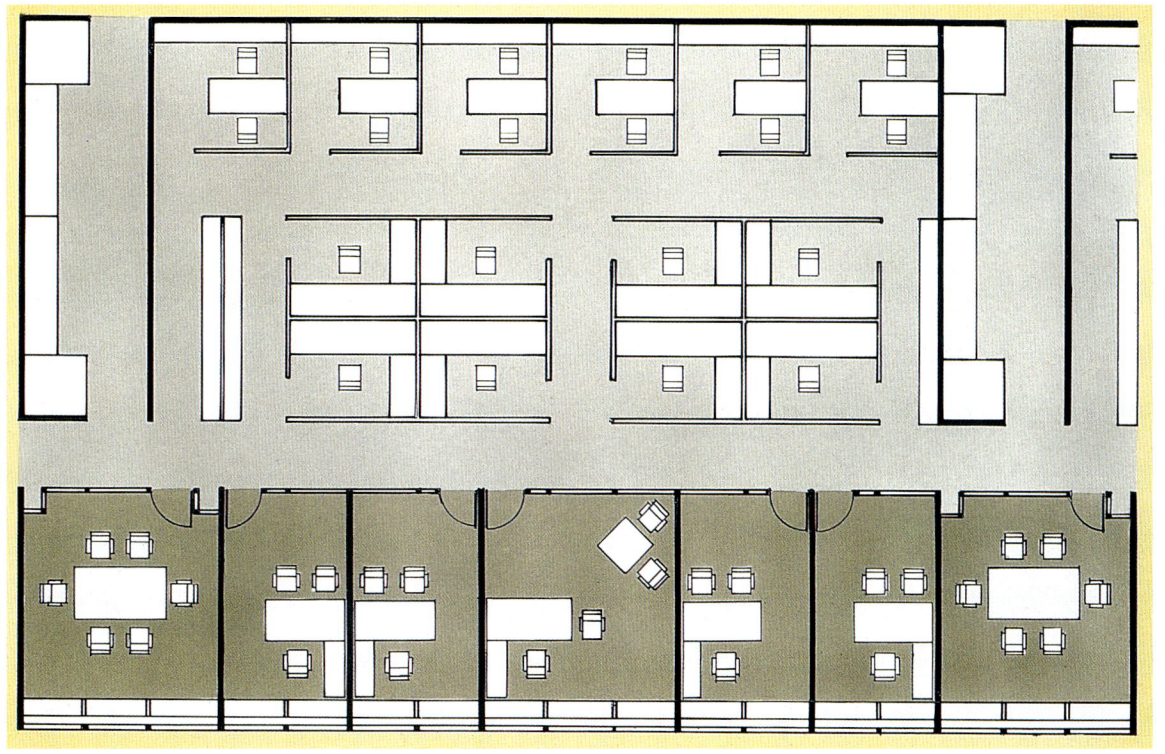

9

101

10 Typical portion of center corridor on office floor.
11 Typical private office, showing indirect lighting fixture below clerestory, standardized modular furniture.
12 Typical open-office workstations, with private offices beyond.
13 Portion of demountable office partition, with clear glass clerestory
14 Doorway to private office, showing glass in partitions.
15 Typical private office along window wall

10

11

12

The bank and the architects worked closely with a major producer of demountable partitions to fill the staff's precise needs. It was important to have a minimum number of standardized partition components. Similarly, with the office furniture, it was essential to minimize the number of different components. During the process, structural column dimensions and systems for office lighting and air supply were refined.

Office lighting was one of several components affected by the limited height of the office floors. The minimal depth above the dropped ceilings ruled out ceiling-recessed lighting, and suspended lighting would have presented unwanted visual obstructions in the low-ceilinged spaces. The concept of partitions with clerestories, however, provided an opportunity to design wall-mounted lighting, set just below the clerestories—ideally situated above eye level yet low enough to allow uniform distribution of indirect light across the ceilings. The potential problem of glare on the wall itself was eliminated because the portion of the partitions above the lights is clear glass.

Every detail of the offices was studied down to a fraction of an inch. With the help of a wood consultant, anagre was selected as the standard veneer for its environmental acceptability, its color, and its subtle contrast with paper on the desktop; more muted grain patterns were used on desktops, to minimize distraction, and stronger ones used on vertical surfaces.

13

14

15

Special Spaces

Auditorium

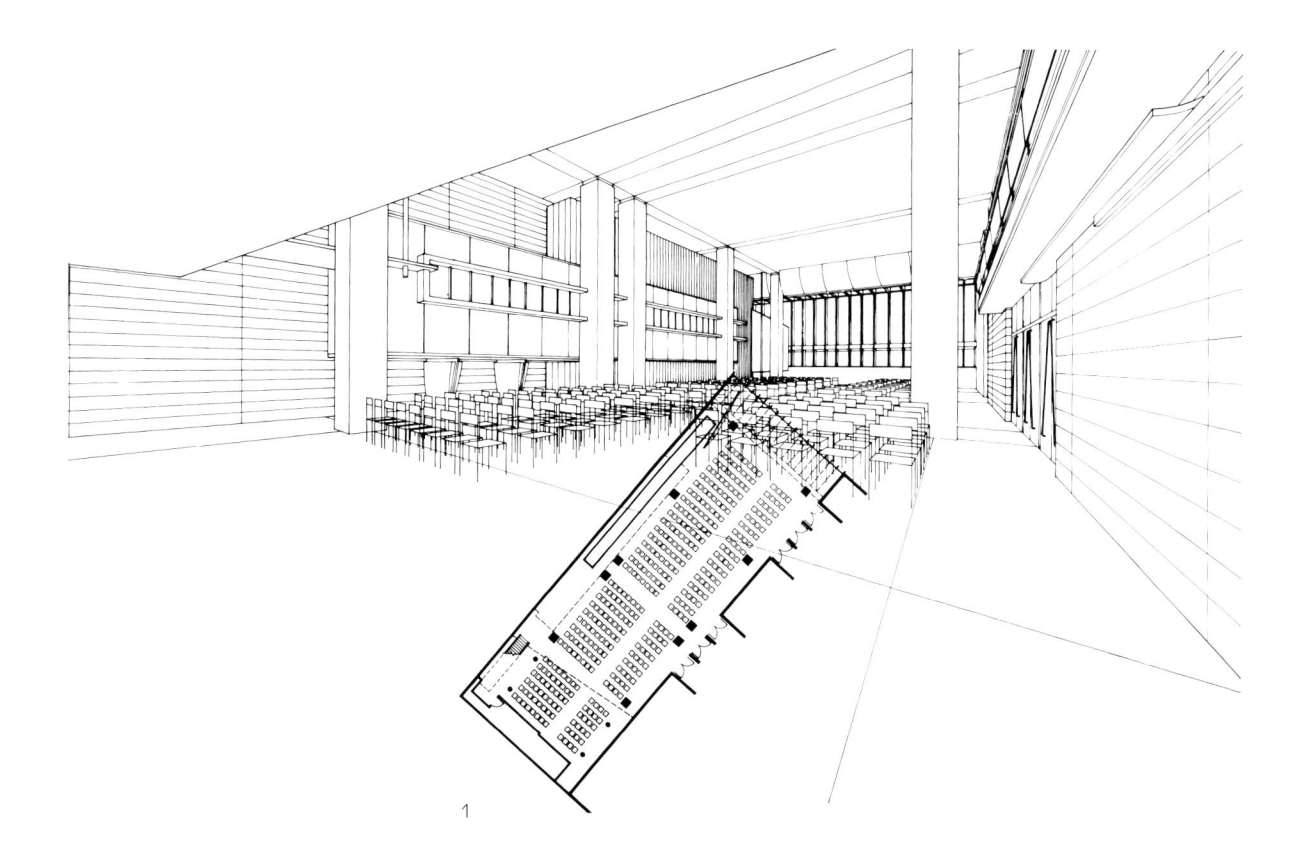

1

The World Bank's architectural program called for three distinctive large-scale meeting places: an auditorium, the Executive Directors' Board Room, and the Executive Directors' Conference Room. For maximum accessibility to bank staff and visitors, the auditorium was located on the main floor, just off the main lobby. A double-height rectangular volume, the room has a long booth for simultaneous translators along one side.

The Board Room and the Conference Room, closely associated with the bank's highest executives, are located on the 13th floor, where they benefit from the city's height limit exemption for the upper parts of rooms. The lofty Board Room is visible from the exterior as a prominent sculptural element crowning the phase one construction at the corner of 18th and H streets. The boat-like shape of its roof structure is visible from blocks away.

Inside, the Board Room is dominated by a horseshoe-shaped table seating 35. Light is diffused throughout the room from a clerestory band just under the ceiling and through a series of vertical windows on axis with the entrance to the room. A band of ornament based on the flags of member nations runs around the space just under the clerestory.

2

The Conference Room has an equally visible role on the exterior of the building, perching at the top of the main entrance front. It is distinguished visually by a wall of vertical fins that fend off late afternoon sun while permitting a full view out across the city's rooftops.

Each of these two top-floor meeting rooms has its own lobby-lounge area, where attendees can mingle, talk in small groups, and make telephone calls. These have comfortable chairs and carpets with distinctive borders designed by KPF, but their principal luxuries are daylight and views out over the city.

1 Perspective drawing and plan of auditorium.
2 Completed auditorium.

Executive Directors' Board Room

3

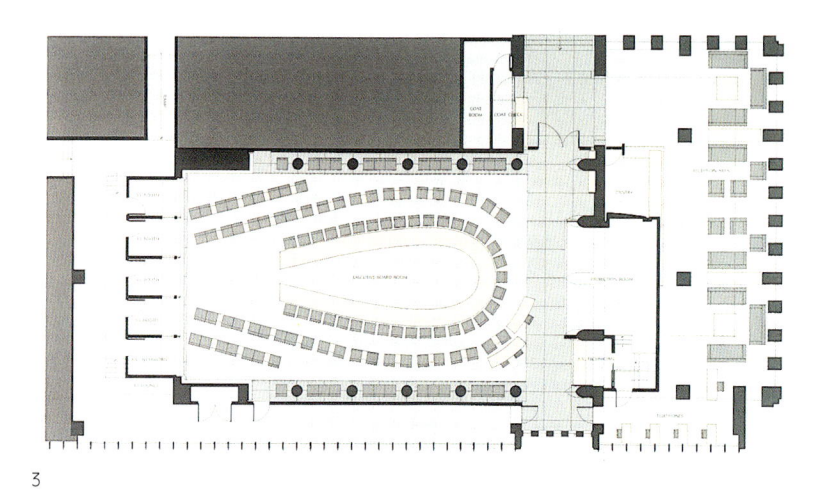

3 Plan of Executive Directors' Board Room, final design.
4 Model of Executive Directors' Board Room, final design.
5 Schematic drawing of major top-floor spaces, Board Room at left and Conference Room at right.
6&7 Section drawings of Executive Directors' Board Room.
8 Exterior model view of Executive Directors' Board Room.

4

5

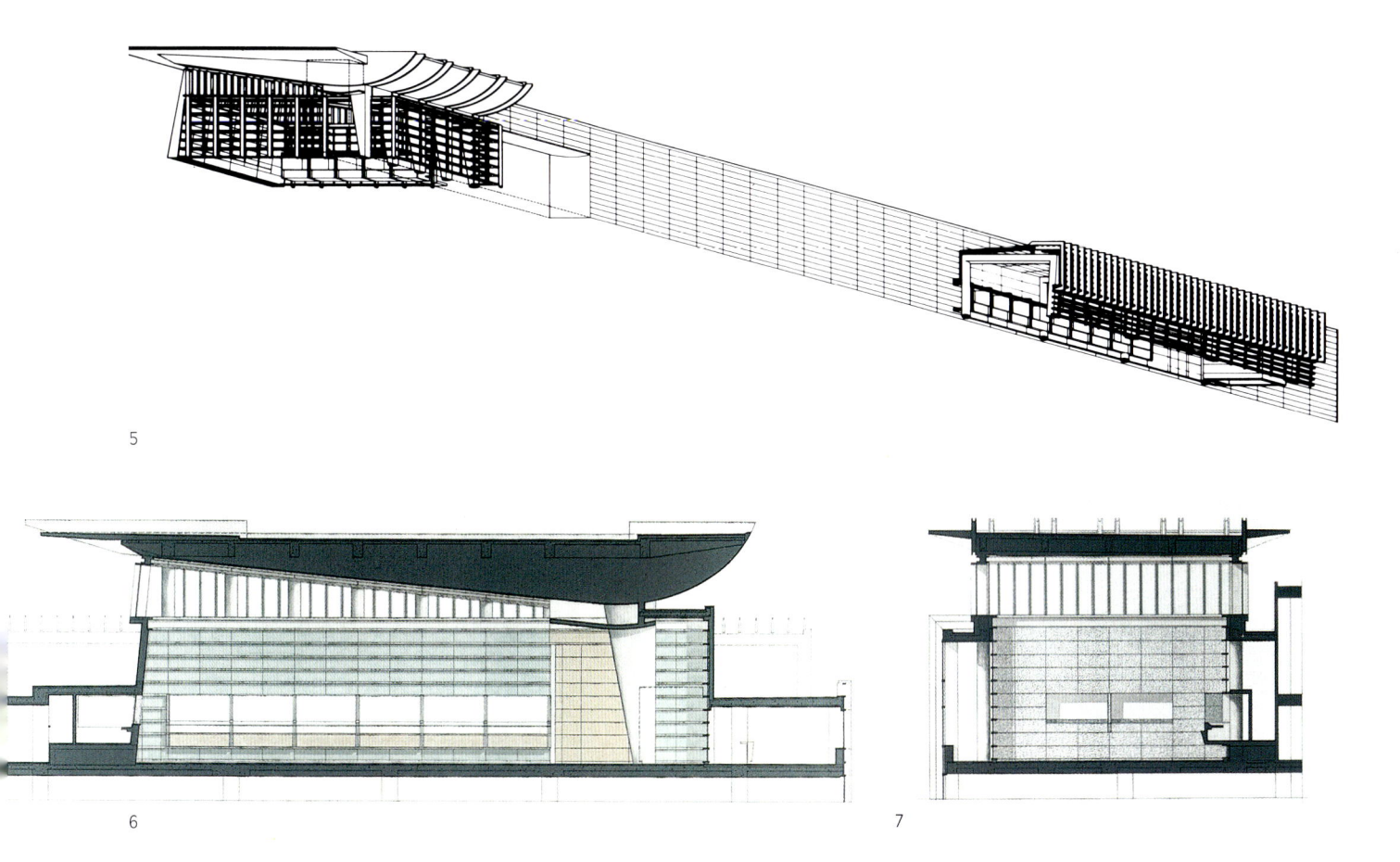

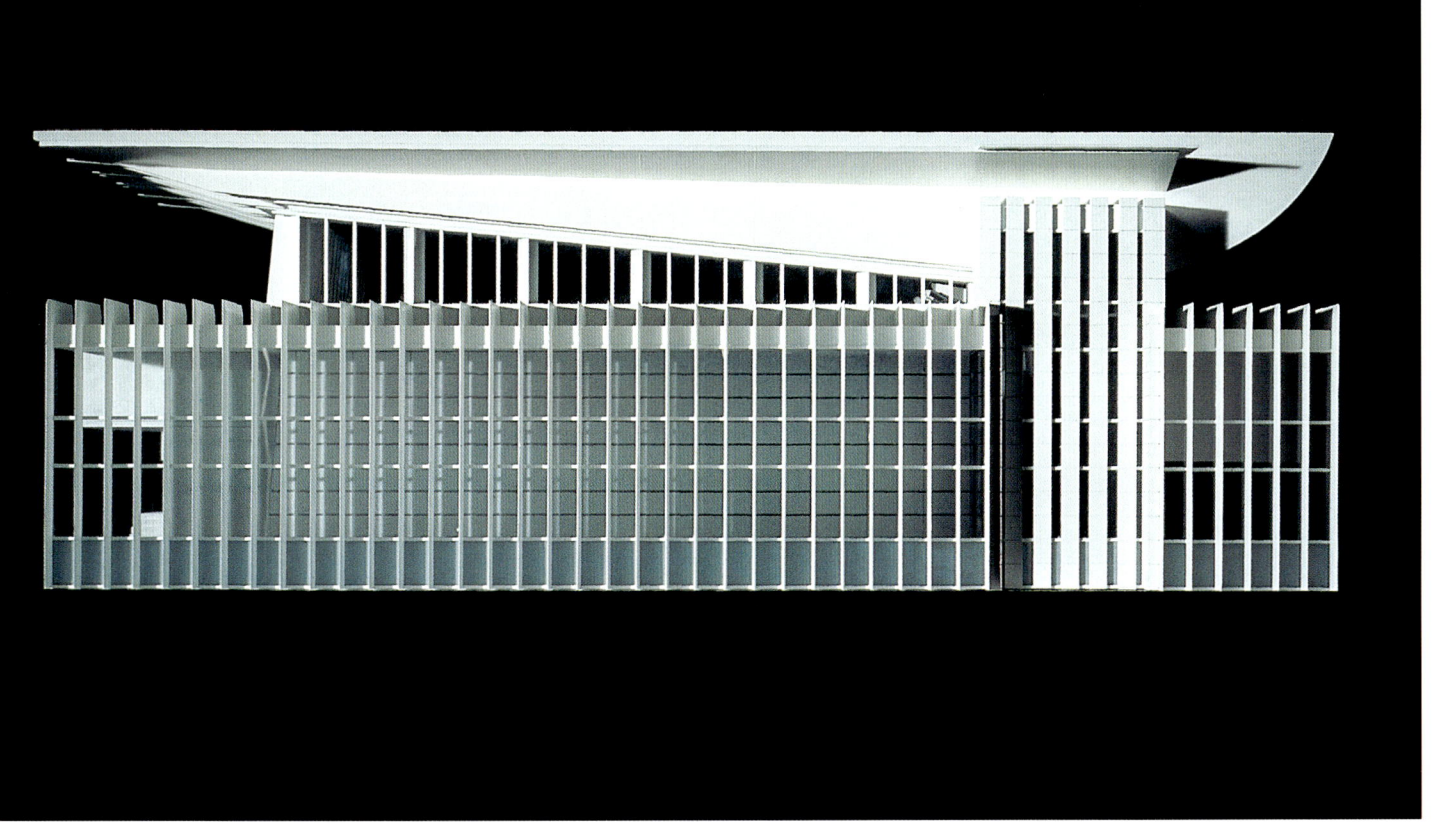

6

7

8

9–11 Three views of the Executive Directors' Board Room, showing horseshoe-shaped table, sculptural ceiling, and frieze based on flags below clerestory.

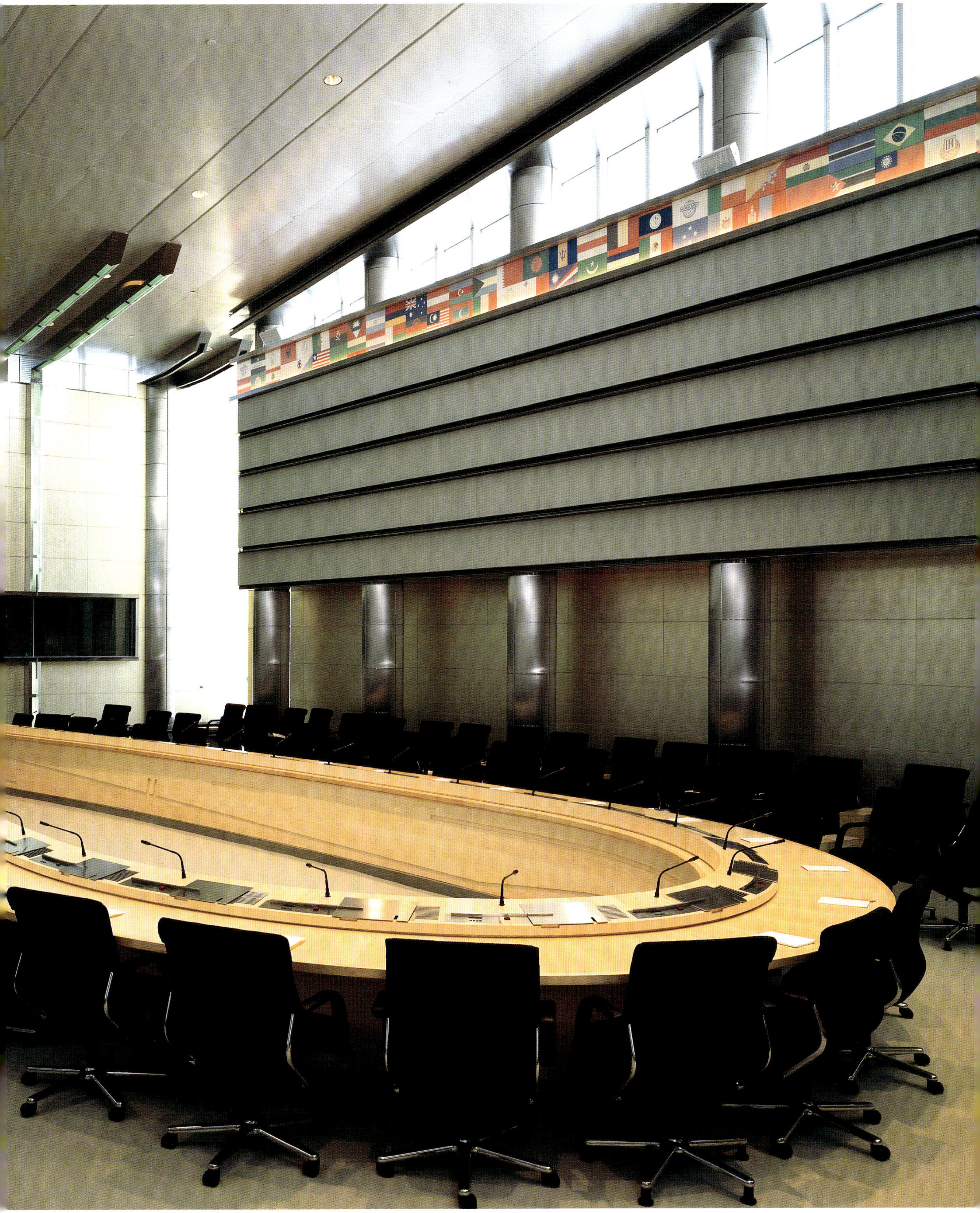

12 Corner of Board Room with one of desks that surround main table.
13 Open end of horseshoe-shaped Boardroom table, showing furniture and carpet details.
14 End of Executive Directors' Boardroom, showing display cases, windows, and lighting.

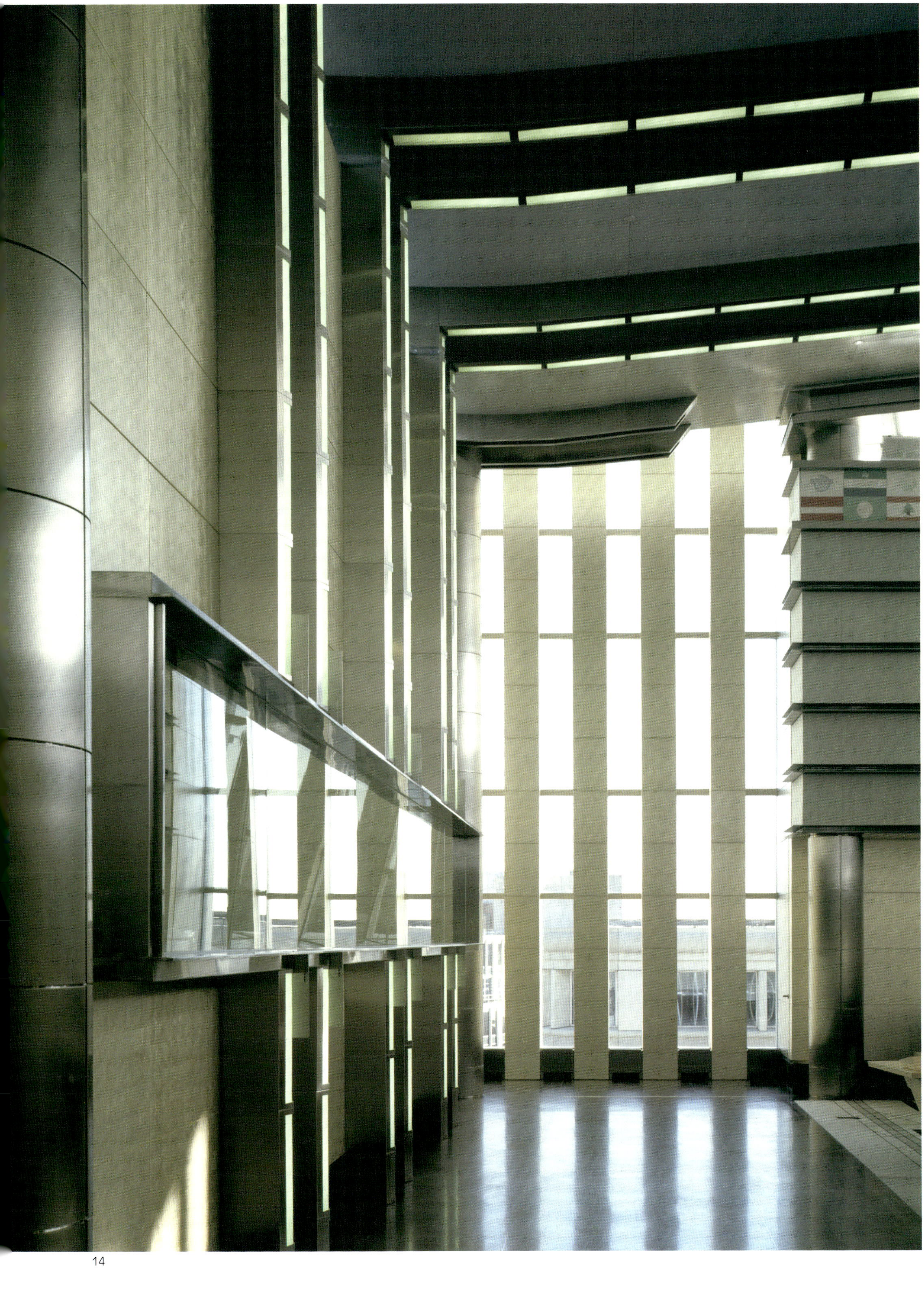

15–18 Four views of Executive Directors' Boardroom lounge, showing details of walls, furniture, and lighting.

15

16

17

18

19 Lounge and reception desk outside Executive Directors' Conference Room.
20 Executive Directors' Conference Room, with extensive windows overlooking Washington rooftops.

Executive Directors' Conference Room

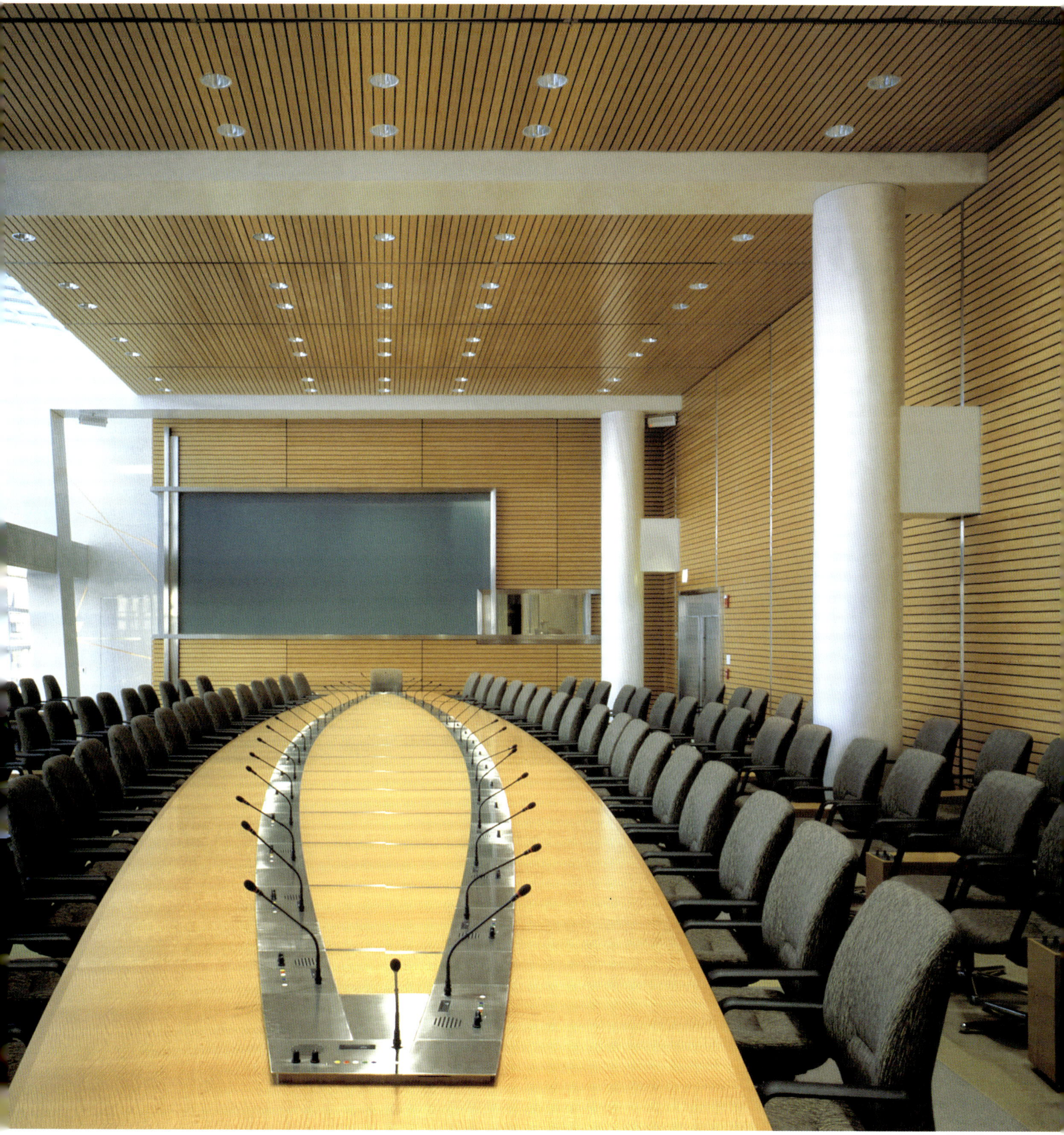

Cafeteria

1

1 View into atrium light well, with cafeteria seen inside glazed wall.
2 Stair down to corridor at cafeteria level, with pool outside glazed wall.
3 Area on route to cafeteria, with view of waterfall in light well.
4 Cafeteria terrace suspended above light well pool.

2

3

4

The World Bank's cafeteria, along with many other facilities shared by all its offices, was destined from the outset to be located below street level. That was an inevitable consequence of fitting the bank's programmed square footage within the city's building height limit. What KPF's design accomplished was to make a virtue of this necessity.

A crucial factor in making the cafeteria appealing is the light well that extends down two stories below the street-level atrium. Situated just under the atrium floor, the cafeteria enjoys a view out into the light well from one story above the pool at its base. The waterfall from an atrium level pool passes by the cafeteria windows.

(The obvious parallel is the view of a waterfall and sunken pool from the underground cafeteria at the nearby National Gallery, on which KPF partner William Pedersen worked as a designer for I.M. Pei & Partners.) Bringing daylight into the cafeteria from above is a row of glazed pyramids, which serve as sculptural elements on the atrium floor as they light the cafeteria. After dark, the artificial lighting in the pyramids helps to illuminate both atrium and cafeteria.

The route of the typical cafeteria patron is a visually appealing sequence. Descending to the first basement level by stair or elevator, the cafeteria-goer proceeds along the glazed walls of the light well, with a well calculated view of

5

6 7

8

9

5 Counters in serving area offering regional cuisines.
6 Cafeteria serving area, with faceted metallic ceiling.
7 Checkout counters in cafeteria serving area.
8 Main seating area of cafeteria.
9 Condiment counters, with seating area of cafeteria beyond translucent partition.

10 Detail of executive dining room.
11 Cafeteria seating alcove.
12 A la carte dining room.
13 Diners in cafeteria alcove.
14 Row of cafeteria seating alcoves.

10

11

12

the waterfall, then goes into a spacious serving area, with soft indirect lighting reflected from faceted ceiling surfaces. More intense light is directed to the food counters.

Emerging from the serving area into the dining area, one experiences somewhat higher overall illumination and sees the light well view from a different angle, behind the waterfall. Seating is provided in a wide variety of configurations, from a relatively wide open central area to intimate alcoves. Generous use of translucent panels adds to a feeling of openness and light. There is also the option of going beyond the cafeteria proper to the tables on a balcony that hovers above the light well pool. The route back to work from the cafeteria crosses a footbridge over the pool, almost close enough to the waterfall to get splashed.

13

14

Other Below-Grade Spaces

1–9 A variety of basement workplaces and employee service spaces.

6

7

9

8

In addition to the cafeteria, the building's below-grade levels house a variety of facilities that serve the entire bank staff, among them libraries, archives, a credit union, a travel bureau, employee health services, a mail room, and a substantial printing operation for the bank's documents and publications. As many of these facilities as possible benefit from exposure to the light well that brings daylight down two stories below the atrium. Some of these facilities extend out under the sidewalks surrounding the building. A portion of the bank's five levels of below-grade space provides parking for 500 cars.

FINISHES/FURNISHINGS

1   Detail of main lobby, showing terrazzo floor and carpet with architect-designed border.
2   Portion of atrium floor, showing terrazzo with glass aggregate and embedded glass block to light spaces below.
3   Buffet dining room finishes
4   Executive Directors' Conference Room finishes
5   Bathroom finishes

3

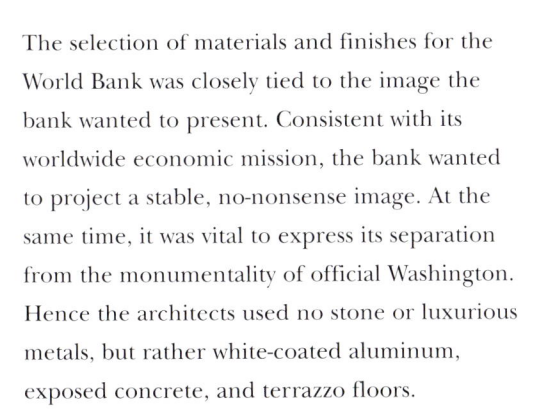

4

5

The selection of materials and finishes for the World Bank was closely tied to the image the bank wanted to present. Consistent with its worldwide economic mission, the bank wanted to project a stable, no-nonsense image. At the same time, it was vital to express its separation from the monumentality of official Washington. Hence the architects used no stone or luxurious metals, but rather white-coated aluminum, exposed concrete, and terrazzo floors.

This did not mean, however, that the building's surfaces had to look by any means ordinary. The concrete of the atrium columns and the curtain wall piers are meticulously crafted, using precise forms to produce distinctive textures.

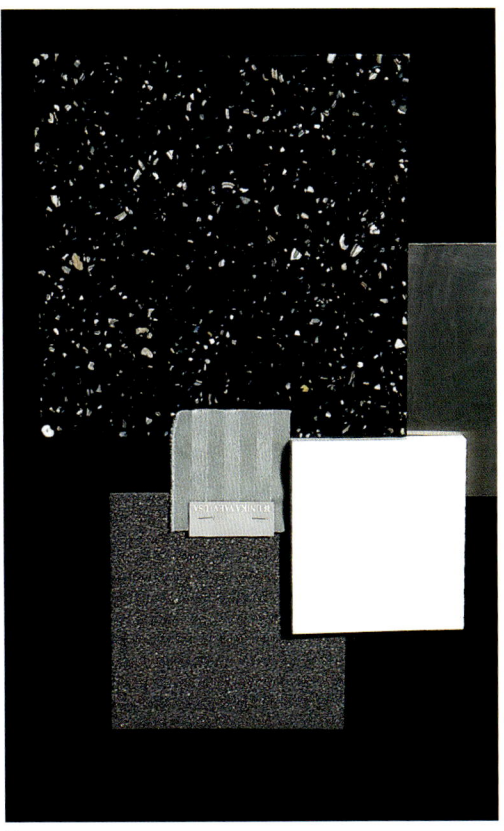

6 Lobby finishes
7 Cafeteria serving area finishes
8 Dining Room finishes
9 Cafeteria finishes

6

7

The terrazzo floors of the lobbies and atrium incorporate clear glass aggregate that produces shimmering refractions when light hits it.

The colors of the exterior and public spaces are held within a narrow range: white and the subtle colors the architects determined for concrete, terrazzo, fabrics, carpets, and glass. These colors were carefully adjusted in a range of cool grays, in contrast to the colors of the two existing buildings—the beige tone of the D Building travertine and the almost taupe gray of the E Building limestone. Since most of the structures in the neighborhood have a warm gray chroma, this building stands out for

appearing somewhat lavender by comparison, with white highlights that are also exceptional in this district.

The major shared spaces of the building—the lobby, the atrium, and the cafeteria—maintain this cool gray color range, reinforced by the aluminum leaf ceiling of the lobby. The elevators have metallic interiors. It is only behind the closed doors of the auditorium, on the office floors, and in the top-floor meeting rooms that the honey tones of anegre and other woods interact with the colors of glass and metals to provide a warmer overall palette.

8

9

ART PROGRAM

1 Above reception desk in lobby, untitled mixed-media wall sculpture by Maricruz Arribas of Peru.
2 *Insect Diskette Series II* by Ahmad Shukri of Malaysia.
3 *Insect Diskette Series II* in place near passage to 18th Street entrance.
4 Installed under central terrace in atrium, *Global Groove* by Nam June Paik of USA and Korea.

Rather than displaying a set of commissioned art works in its new headquarters, the World Bank decided to pursue an art program more in keeping with its mission. It has been organizing and expanding a collection of works from many of its 182 member nations and distributing them throughout the building. In the first-floor lobbies and atrium, some of these works are more or less permanently installed, and special temporary works are occasionally installed.

The World Bank's art program began back in the 1970s as a conventional program for adorning the offices with selected art. Committees of bank staff, sometimes working with outside consultants, made some fine acquisitions. Notably among these is the collection of traditional African art assembled in the early 1980s, when the bank completed a building specifically for its African operations.

No specific installations were planned for the new building before it opened. When it was completed, the existing Art Committee and newly elected bank president James Wolfensohn supported the establishment of an official Art Program. Artemis Zenetou, a curator with museum experience, was hired to direct it. Her tasks included care and management of the existing collection, as well as a new acquisitions program. The program includes state-of-the-art storage facilities for works not currently on display. Altogether, says Zenetou, the program has the scope and scale of a medium-size museum.

It was agreed from the outset that the objective of the Art Program was not to decorate the building, but to assemble works related to the bank's worldwide social and economic missions, while contributing to an aesthetically and intellectually stimulating work environment. The Art Program is charged with acquiring, exhibiting, and maintaining contemporary art from member nations in all geographical regions.

Particular attention is given to encouraging emerging artists in developing countries. Zenetou and her staff work with curators, art professionals, and organizations throughout the world to identify artworks and projects for the collection. Efforts are made to promote work by the selected artists in the international art market. The World Bank Collection, says Zenetou, is "not only about investing in art but also about investing in people—the artists who create it."

The growing art collection is displayed in the bank's public spaces and in senior management offices. The "public" locations include lobbies, elevator waiting areas, the atrium, conference rooms, and private dining rooms. Many of these are hospitable to art display, and the corridor walls on the office floors provide exceptionally generous display areas. Most of the collection is organized by country or geographical region, and collections rotate between floors and other World Bank buildings.

2

3

4

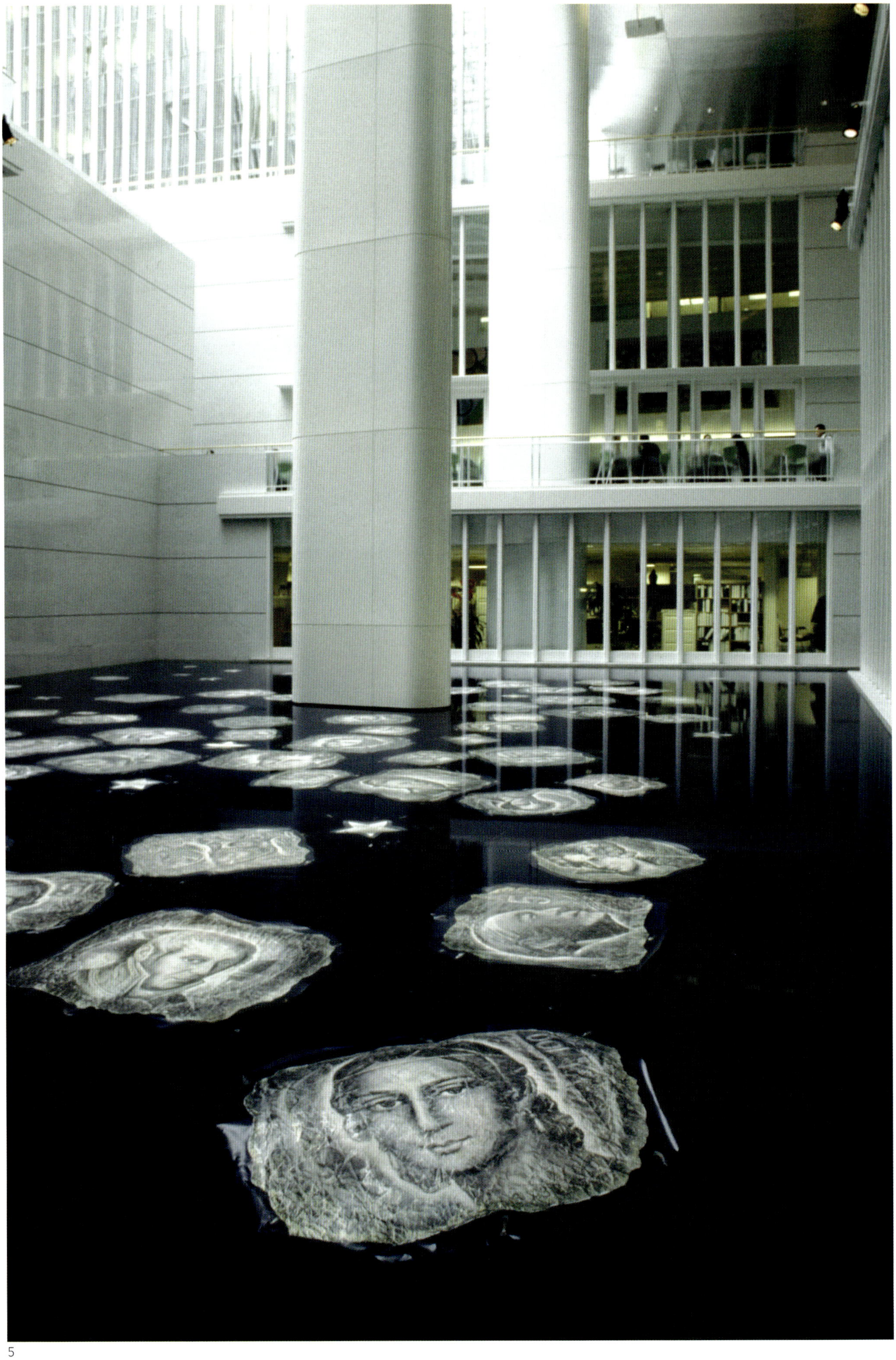

5

In addition to exhibits of the permanent collection, the building houses occasional site-specific installations that deal with current issues. An example of such a temporary exhibition was the use of the atrium reflecting pool for an installation commemorating the emergence of the Euro currency. Entitled Goodbye Favorite European Portraits: Hello Euro, the work by Moscow artists Valera and Natasha Cherkashin immersed waterproof images from the outgoing bank notes in the pool. It was meant to challenge established notions about art and how it is displayed, and it attracted much attention in the international press. Such works, says Zenetou, "invite the visitor to look at both the art and the space in different ways."

5 Temporarily installed in pool at base of light well, *Goodbye Favorite European Portraits: Hello Euro* by Russian artists Valera and Natasha Cherkashin, based on currency to be replaced by the euro.
6 Installed on wall behind security desk, images from *Goodbye Favorite European Portraits: Hello Euro*.
7 Detail of *Fishes* by Yorgos Kypris of Cyprus, with one bronze fish for each of 182 World Bank members.
8 *Fishes*, bronze and iron wall sculpture by Yorgos Kypris, installed in 19th Street entrance lobby.

9 *Athletic Games* by Adamu of Ethiopia.
10 In typical office floor corridor, untitled work by Thi Tham Poong Dinh of Vietnam in foreground.
11 Three works by Chant Avedissian of Egypt: *Mohatta Masr Central Station*; *Share' Mohamad Ali, Cairo*; *Om Kasloum*.
12 Top-floor lobby with, at left, *Solidarity* by Dolorosa Sinaga of Indonesia and, at right, *Ambiance de Marche* by Viyé Diba of Senegal.

9

10

11

12

FINAL EVALUATION

1 Banquet in World Bank atrium.

The completed World Bank has rewarded the scrupulous work of the bank staff and the design team by serving as an exceptionally effective headquarters. Employees are happy to work here, and visitors are pleased with its gracious spaces. As Gene Kohn characterizes the building: "It has a balance between dignity and economy that is appropriate to this institution. It has a clarity of organization. And the atrium at its heart says, 'Here is where the world comes together'."

An important goal from the outset was to avoid any sense of opulence or waste, and the completed building's primary features are well organized spaces and beautifully modulated light, rather than rich materials. The luxuries of the building are the atrium space and the daylight it admits, which are cost effective over the life of the building. And the atrium lends spaciousness and light to all the areas around it. The underground cafeteria, for instance, by nature an economical facility, gains light and views from the atrium.

The building's elegance has been achieved without the use of natural stone, fine metals, or rare woods. What we see instead are aluminum, synthetic floors (given a visually luxurious texture with embedded glass fragments), and concrete surfaces refined by careful but economical fabrication methods. The bank expresses refinement with no suggestion of lavishness.

The atrium has turned out to be a superb setting for events sponsored by the bank and others: an American Institute of Architects banquet, a D.C. film festival gala, an international development "marketplace," the bank's informational exhibits, and so on. Such uses were uncommon in the building's first year, perhaps because of concerns that the new headquarters would be seen as too opulent. But the atrium and the building as a whole are not luxurious except in the outstanding spaces the architects have been able to provide. Though not a requirement for the bank's operation, the atrium is paying for itself in reduced annual energy costs for surrounding functions. Its austere palette of materials and colors effectively complements events held within it.

As it gained experience with the new building, the bank introduced an employee café to the atrium mezzanine, which adds welcome activity to the space. Also added have been some ficus trees, which the architects had felt would be superfluous, to make the space more hospitable.

1

2   View from north, with Pennsylvania Avenue, small park, and H Street in foreground, 19th Street at right.
Following pages: World Bank at night, with 18th Street at left, Pennsylvania Avenue in immediate foreground.

Seyda Kocer, an architect on the bank's staff who worked closely with KPF on the building's design, reports that she gives many tours of the building. She finds visitors particularly impressed with the quality and distinctiveness of the details: the floor coverings, the fabrics on the dining room chairs, the patterns on the elevator doors and cabs, the signage. As a reference for any future alterations, she keeps samples in her office of specified wood, glass, metal, and other items that contribute to the building's identity.

The World Bank superbly meets the needs—functional and symbolic—of its owner, and that is cause for celebration. But the building goes beyond that to set an example for the larger world of architecture and urban development. It deals successfully with major issues that Modern architects have been wrestling with for a century.

At the local level, the World Bank sets an example for dealing with the special circumstances of Washington, D.C. It is one of the few Washington landmarks of recent decades that shows full respect for the city's special texture without adopting its pervasive Neo-Classical trappings. It joins the exalted company of the D.C. Metro stations (1976 to present), the East Building of the National Gallery by I.M. Pei & Partners (1978) and the Vietnam Memorial by Maya Lin (1982).

Beyond the particular circumstances of Washington, however, the building is an object lesson in expressing the importance of an organization without resorting to heavy-handed symbolism. The world is full of governmental and quasi-governmental buildings that look too pompous, too forbidding, or simply too utilitarian for their place in society. The World Bank looks like an office building, but an office building with a larger purpose that goes beyond the private and the lucrative.

The building's exterior respects the streets of the city. Its envelope is assembled of practical elements that are at the scale of Washington's office buildings, not its government landmarks. Its principal front forms a finely tuned backdrop for the modest public space it faces. The main entrance is emphatic but by no means overstated.

The exhilaration of the World Bank's atrium, expressing the international scale of its activities, is wisely reserved for the interior. As on the outside, there is nothing pompous—just a very large, light-filled volume, with a few large-scaled elements supporting its roof and numerous smaller features relating to the scale of the occupants. It is an excellent example of the use of the atrium to meet the needs of a large urban building.

Another absolutely crucial lesson of the World Bank is the way it amalgamates old and new structures to produce a whole that is more than a mere clash of parts. The expansion of organizations within our established cities regularly involves the decision to save or demolish older structures. Extending the useful life of older structures is, of course, the responsible strategy to take, but that can often result in serious functional and aesthetic compromises. KPF's unique qualification to undertake this project was its proposal to save some earlier buildings , and the result is a lesson to other architects about absorbing existing structures into a larger whole—a whole that not only accepts them, but is positively affected by their presence.

In its concept and in its details, the World Bank merits the attention of architects and their prospective clients the world over.

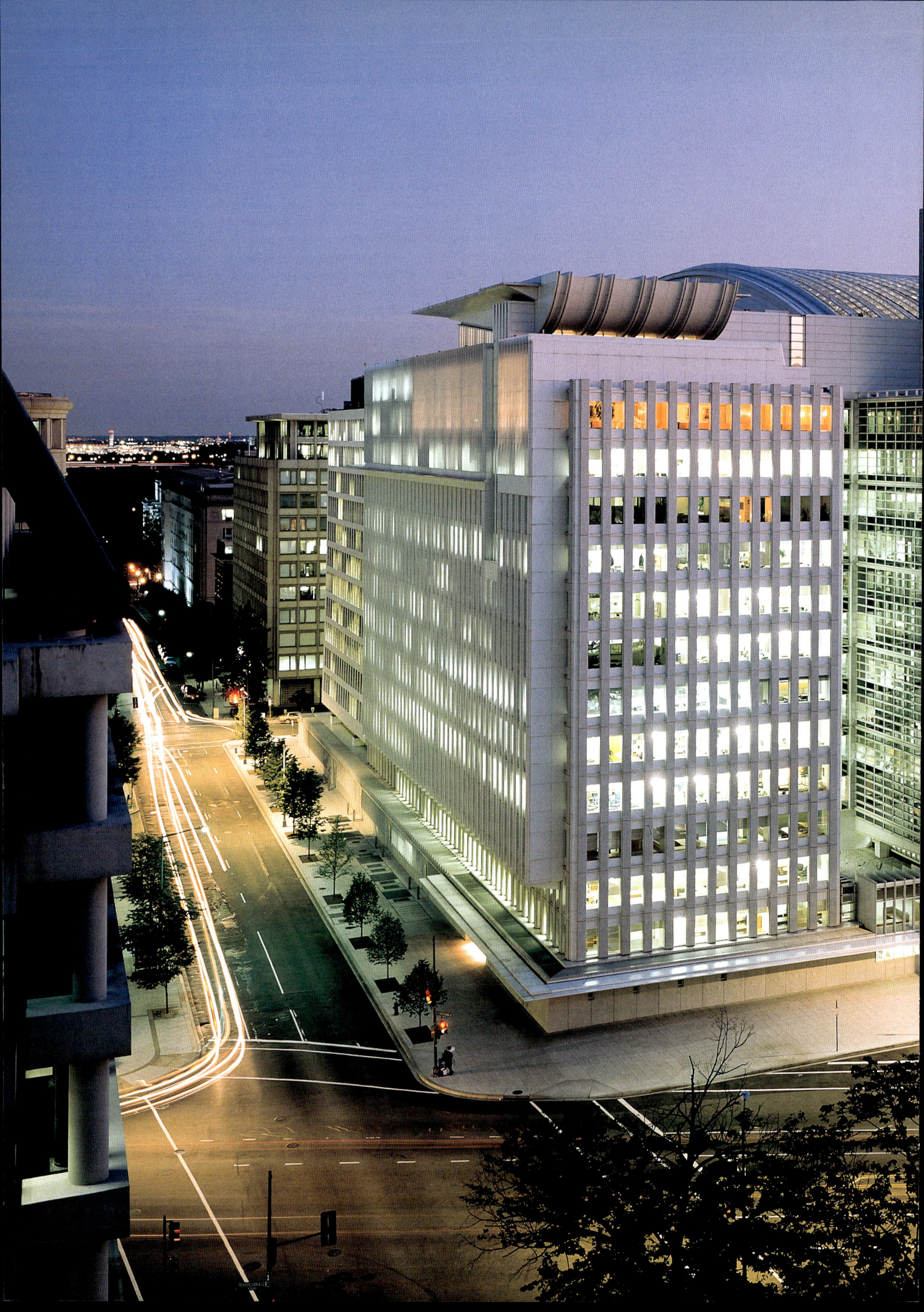

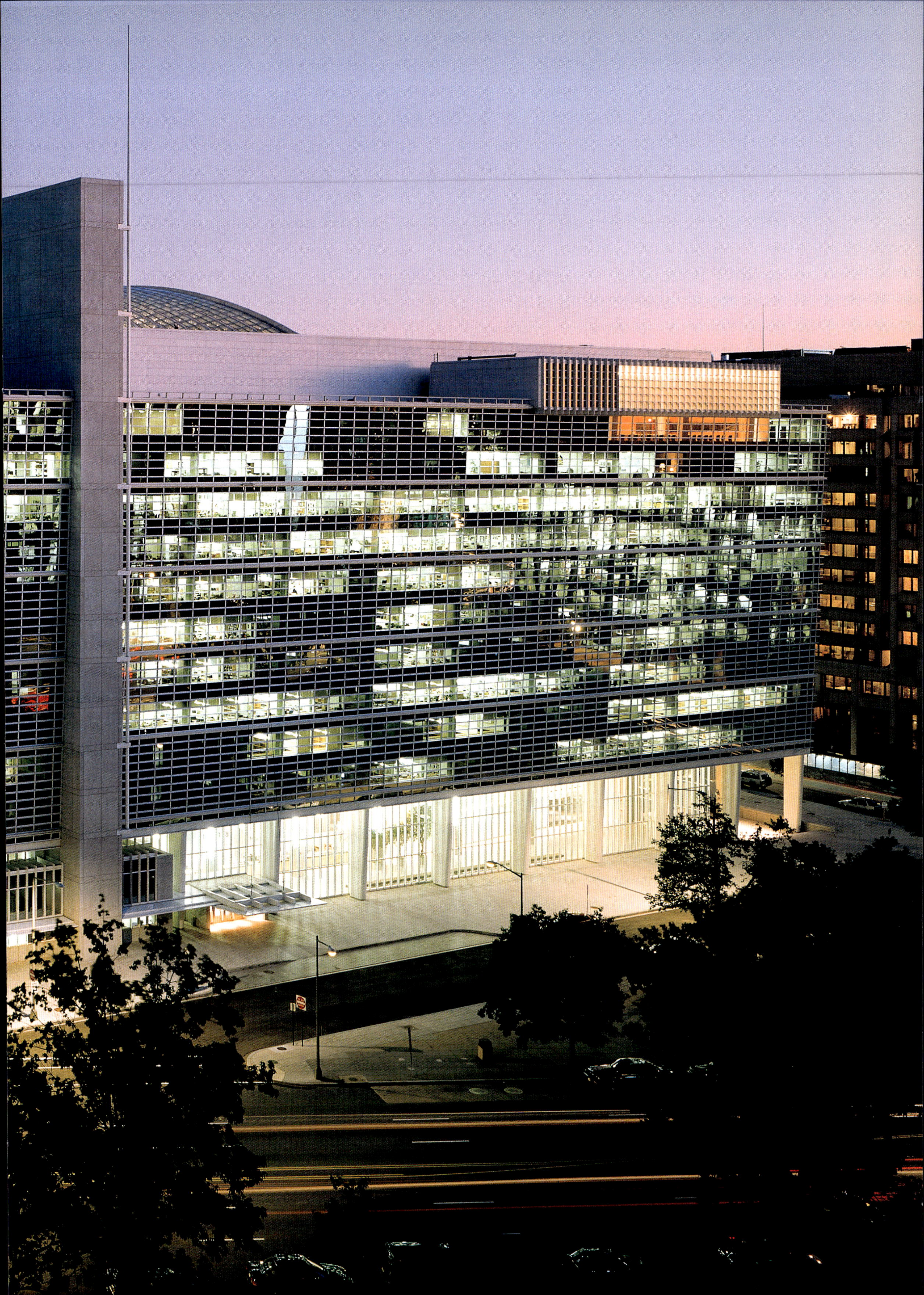

4 World Bank atrium roof seen in distant skyline view.

4

Credits

Client: The International Bank for Reconstruction and Development (The World Bank), Washington, DC.

> **Director, Headquarters Construction Department:** Ernesto E. Henriod
>
> **Chief HQC Major Projects Division:** Peter Copplestone.
>
> **Facilities Design:** Hisao Kimura, Seyda Kocer, Jonathan Lyttle, Naoto Oka.
>
> **Implementation Unit:** Douglas B. Hatch, Pat Hennessy, Els Hinderdael-Forger, Steve LaRoche.

Architects: Kohn Pedersen Fox Associates, Architects and Planning Consultants, New York.

> **Partners-in-Charge:** A. Eugene Kohn, Sheldon Fox.
>
> **Design Partner:** William Pedersen.
>
> **Senior Designer:** Craig Nealy.
>
> **Project Manager:** (Phase I): William H. Cunningham, (Phase II): Thomas Holzmann.
>
> **Coordination Leader:** Joseph P. Ruocco.
>
> **Project Team:** Isabelle Autones, Dayo Babalola, Vladimir Balla, Joseph Barnes, Suzanne Cregan, Eric Daum, Dominic Dunn, Valerie Edozien, Armando Gutierrez, Fia Hekmat, Michael Martin, Hun Oh, Paul Regan, Duncan Reid, James Seger, Frank Shenton, David Thompson, Thomas Vandenbout.
>
> **Contributors:** Robin Andrade, Pavel Balla, Mark Barnhouse, Gabrielle Blackman, Larry Cohen, Nathan Corser, Cynthia Crier, Glen DaCosta, Anthony DiGrazia, Mark Fiedler, Robin Goldberg, Koichiro Ishiguro, Tatiana Kasnar, Sulan Kolatan, Judy Lee, Ming Leung, Jenny Ling, Kristen Minor, Nicole Mronz, Beth Niemi, Steve Ott, Jim Papoutsis, Peter Schubert, Esmatollah Seraj, Audrey Shen, Emil Stojakovitch, John Stoltze, Hisaya Sugiyama.

Interior Architect: KPF Interior Architects, New York.

> **Partner-in-Charge:** Robert Cioppa.
>
> **Project Team:** Gustavo Matticolli, Ruxandra Panaitescu, Keith Rosen, Jorge Septian, George Sucato.

Associated Architect: Kresscox Associates, Washington, DC.

> **Partners:** David Cox, Jerrily R. Kress.
>
> **Project Team:** Cristoffer A. Graae, Joanna Schmickel, Diana Gonzalez.

Construction Manager: Sverdrup Hanscomb Gilbane. Zahid Babar, Tom Cohn, Bob DeWolfe, Darick Edmond, Merrill Lambert, Mark Mathieson, Larry Rebel Preston Rivers, Hazel Snowden.

Solicitor: Bernstein, Weiss, Coplan, Weinstein & Lake, New York. Norman Coplan.

Structural Engineer: Weidlinger Associates, New York.

> **Partner:** Matthys Levy.
>
> **Senior Associate:** Maurice Zilberstein.

Mechanical Engineer: Flack & Kurtz, New York.

> **Principals:** Norman D. Kurtz, Henry DiGregorio, Vincent Campanella, George Santonas, Walter Cooper.
>
> **Project team:** Joseph Morrongiello, Arthur Mehlman, Alex Alijewicz, Felix Mejia, Bob Bonn, Marty Cassidy.

Vertical Transportation/Materials Handling: John A. Van Deusen & Associates, Livingston, NJ. John A. Van Deusen, Ahmet Tanyen.

Traffic Consultants: Gorove, Slade & Associates, Washington, DC. Louis Slade, Frederick E. Gorove.

Cost Estimating: V. J. Associates, West Babylon, NY. Vijay Desai.

Food Service/Laundry/Solid Waste: Cini-Little International, Rockville, MD. William V. Eaton, Thomas Cason.

Civil Engineering: Loierderman Associates, Lanham, MD.

> **Vice President:** Paul Oscar.
>
> **Associates:** Joseph Hines, Melvin Willis.

Security: Booz-Allen & Hamilton, Seabrook, MD. Richard Tatum, Jim Black.

Acoustical Consultants/Audiovisual: Shen Milsom & Wilke, New York. Fred Shen, Nick Assadourian, Steven Emspak, James Merrill.

Lighting Consultant: Kugler Tillotson Associates, New York. Jerry Kugler, Suzanne Tillotson, Mark Kubicki.

Fire Protection Engineers: Rolf Jensen & Associates, Springfield, NJ.

> **Vice President:** John McCormick. Joseph Hauf.

Window Washing/Building Maintenance: High Rise Systems, Fort Worth, TX. David Jaffe.

Landscape: Rhodeside & Harwell, Alexandria, VA.
Faye B. Harwell.

Fountain Consultant: William Hobbs, Ltd., Atlanta, GA.
William Hobbs.

Graphic Designer: Carbone Smolan Associates, New York.
Ken Carbone, Claire Taylor.

Specifications: Heller & Metzger, Washington, DC.
Barbara Heller.

General Contractor: The George Hyman Construction Co., Washington, DC.

Field Office: Peter Chase, Alex Palacios, Tracy Brown, Dan Sennewald, Jim Merlene.

Site Office: George Morrison, Kelley Wallace.

Curtainwall Contractors: Harmon Contract W.S.A., Columbia, MD.
Larry A. Lough, Jana Ash, Tim Dunn.

Precast Contractor: Pre-Con Company, Brampton, Ontario, Canada.
Leo Angelantoni.

Elevator Contractor: Otis Elevator Company, Alexandria, VA.
Ralph Valentino.

Mechanical Contractor: John J. Kirlin, Inc., Washington, DC.
Project Manager: Frank Williams, Sr.

Electrical Contractor: Dynalectric, Washington, DC.
Project Manager: George Minor.

Sheet Metal Contractor: United Sheet Metal, Capitol Heights, MD.
Project Manager: Joe Batch.

Fire Protection Contractor: National Fire Protection, Rockville, MD.
Project Manager: George Buell.

Photography

Michael Dersin: cover; p.2; p.17 (11); p.18–19 (13); p.24 (1), (2), (3), (4); p.25 (5), (6), (7); p.44–45 (34); p.48–49 (38); p.71 (m); p.74–75 (2), (3); p.76 (6); p.77 (8), (9); p.81; p.87; p.88, p.89 (15); p.90 (16), (17); p.91 (18); p.94 (21), (22); p.96–97 (25); p.102 (10); p.114–115 (19), (20); p.116 (1); p.118 (5), (6), (7), (8), (9); p.121 (14); p.124 (1)

Timothy Hursley: p.12–13 (3); p.14–15 (5); p.46–47, p.84 (8); p.85 (9); p.86 (10); p.92–93 (19), (20); p.138–139

John Hall: p.108–109 (10), (11); p.110 (12), (13); p.111 (14); p.112–113 (15), (16), (17), (18)

R. Latoff Photos: p.14 (4); p.17 (9), (10), (12); p.48 (37); p.136 (2); p.141

Dennis Gilbert architectural photography: p.65 (3)

Jeff D. Goldman: p.128 (1); p.129 (2), (3), (4); p.130 (5); p.131 (6), (7), (8); p.132 (9), (10); p.133 (11), (12)

Richard Payne FAIA: p.65 (5)

Wayne N. T. Fujii: p.65 (4)

Jock Pottle/Esto: p.10-11 (1); p.64 (1); p.25 (8); p.31 (6), (7), (8); p.38 (22), (23), (24); p.39 (25), (26), (27); p.40 (28); p.41 (29); p.82 (5); p.106 (3), (4); p.107 (8); p.125 (3), (5); p.126 (7); p.127 (9)

Don F. Wong Photography: p.64 (2)

Elliot Kaufman: p.102–103 (11), (12), (13), (14)

M. Ianacci: p.5; p.135 (1)

Brian Nolan: p.25 (8); p.31 (6), (7), (8)

Model Makers

Awad Architectural Models Inc.: p.10–11; p.25 (8); p.31 (6), (7), (8); p.38 (22), (23), (24); p.39 (25), (26), (27); p.40 (28); p.41 (29); p.82 (5)

Renderer

Joseph Stashkevetch: p.11 (2); p.42 (30); p.43 (32), (33); 78–79; p.83 (6)

Note: All other material not listed was done by Kohn Pedersen Fox Associates, Architects

Acknowledgments

The number and variety of people who have thoughtfully contributed to this book reflects the complexity of the World Bank Headquarters itself.

Among those at Kohn Pedersen Fox Associates who provided invaluable information and insight were partners A. Eugene Kohn, William Pedersen, and project manager Thomas Holzmann. Exceptionally helpful as well were retired partner Sheldon Fox, former associate partner Craig Nealy, and former KPF staff member Joseph P. Ruocco, who was the firm's job captain for the World Bank.

Assembling all graphics and collaborating on the layout of the book was KPF's Creative Director, Ilona Rider, who also took some excellent photographs that appear in the book. Her assistants, Puja Kutwal and Richard McDonald, lent vital support in generating and assembling graphics.

Providing the opportunity to publish this book was The Images Publishing Group, whose patience and professionalism shown during the production is greatly appreciated.

Several members of the World Bank's Facilities Management Division provided essential information and graphic material. Among them were: Jonathan Lyttle, Seyda Kocer, Naoto Oka, Hisao Kimura, Douglas B. Hatch, Jim Duvall, Patricia Sullivan, and Peter Copplestone. Artemis Zenetou provided briefing and photographs documenting the bank's art program, which she directs.

Helpful information and perspective were provided by David Cox and Joanna Schmickel of KressCox Architects, associated architects for the project.

Among the consultants for the building, Norman Kurtz, of Flack & Kurtz, and Matthys Levy, of Weidlinger Associates, were generous with their time and insights.

All of these individuals did their best to explain the design, construction, and operation of the World Bank Headquarters to me, and in no way are they responsible for any errors that may be found in this book.

John Morris Dixon, FAIA

Every effort has been made to trace the original source of copyright material contained in this book. The publishers would be pleased to hear from copyright holders to rectify any error or omissions.

The information and illustrations in this publication have been prepared and supplied by Kohn Pedersen Fox Associates, Architects. While all reasonable efforts have been made to ensure accuracy, the publishers do not, under any circumstances, accept responsibility for errors, omissions and representations express or implied.